P9-DEQ-730

Praise for *Candy Girl:*

"Cody's prose snaps like a garter belt. . . . good, frothy fun. . . . Diablo Cody is the Mars Rover on the far side of the tip rail, sending back uncannily clear images of life on another planet. For those of us who have stared, transfixed, from a distance, wondering how the air is up there, *Candy Girl* is a bracing lungful."　　　　　　　　　　　　　—*Los Angeles Times*

"[Cody is] a quick, erudite and funny writer. . . . One hell of a good story."　　　　　　　　　　　　　　　　—*Time Out Chicago*

"An inspiration to any woman who's ever gotten her groove on sans clothes in front of her bedroom mirror, Cody's memoir is a seductive thrill and a treat for all."　　　　　　　　—*Playgirl*

". . . a tale alternately titillating, pensive, comical, and occasionally gross."　　　　　　　　　　　　　　　—*New York Post*

". . . flat-out funny and refreshingly devoid of moral conclusions."　　　　　　　　　　　—*Star Tribune* (Minneapolis)

"[H]er greatest talent lies in her ability to expose the lowest of low-culture leanings in prose that alternates between the raunchy and the intellectual. . . . Even if *Candy Girl* lays bare some not-so-sweet realities of the seedier side of exotic dancing, at the very least, this highly readable, hard-gyrating memoir will certainly heat up a few frigid January nights."　　　　—*The Kansas City Star*

". . . a glorious case of Too Much Information."　　　　　　　　　　　　　　　　　—*City Pages* (Minneapolis)

". . . a unique, eye-opening account of her one-year stint as a stripper."　　　　　　　　　　　　　　　—*Complete Woman*

"[S]o alarmingly entertaining, readers will wish the book were longer. . . ."　　　　　　　　　　　　—*Publishers Weekly*

"Cody's lively romp through the adult entertainment business is bound to appeal to those wanting a peek inside the inner workings of the sex industry." —*Booklist*

"Diablo Cody is to stripping what Chuck Klosterman is to pop culture and Sarah Vowell is to American History—an off-kilter visionary cynical enough to trust and talented enough to blister all that her mighty pen touches. *Candy Girl* is fiendishly funny, muscle-car fast, and frighteningly—and I do mean frighteningly—accurate. Lock up your daughters and get your lighters in the air, for *Candy Girl* proves Ms. Diablo to be a writer of rock-star caliber."

—Lily Burana, author, *Strip City: A Stripper's Farewell Journey Across America*

© Scott Walker

Diablo Cody is a freelance journalist and is currently the associate arts editor for *City Pages*, Minneapolis's alternative weekly, where she writes articles on pop culture and film reviews. She's currently working on three screenplays, one currently in production with Mandate Pictures, and two with Warner Bros. She lives in Minneapolis with her husband.

CANDY GIRL

A YEAR IN THE LIFE OF
AN UNLIKELY STRIPPER

DIABLO CODY

GOTHAM
BOOKS

GOTHAM BOOKS
Published by Penguin Group (USA) Inc.
375 Hudson Street, New York, New York 10014, U.S.A.

Penguin Group (Canada), 90 Eglinton Avenue East, Suite 700, Toronto, Ontario,
Canada M4P 2Y3 (a division of Pearson Penguin Canada Inc.); Penguin Books Ltd,
80 Strand, London WC2R 0RL, England; Penguin Ireland, 25 St Stephen's Green,
Dublin 2, Ireland (a division of Penguin Books Ltd); Penguin Group (Australia), 250
Camberwell Road, Camberwell, Victoria 3124, Australia (a division of Pearson
Australia Group Pty Ltd); Penguin Books India Pvt Ltd, 11 Community Centre,
Panchsheel Park, New Delhi–110 017, India; Penguin Group (NZ), Cnr Airborne and
Rosedale Roads, Albany, Auckland, New Zealand (a division of Pearson New Zealand
Ltd); Penguin Books (South Africa) (Pty) Ltd, 24 Sturdee Avenue, Rosebank,
Johannesburg 2196, South Africa

Penguin Books Ltd, Registered Offices: 80 Strand, London WC2R 0RL, England

Published by Gotham Books, a division of Penguin Group (USA) Inc.

Previously published as a Gotham Books hardcover edition, 2006

First trade paperback printing, January 2007

10

Copyright © 2006 by Diablo Cody
All rights reserved

Gotham Books and the skyscraper logo are trademarks of Penguin Group (USA) Inc.

ISBN: 978-1-592-40182-1

Printed in the United States of America
Set in Mrs. Eaves with CgDavison Americana
Designed by Sabrina Bowers

Without limiting the rights under copyright reserved above, no part of this publication
may be reproduced, stored in or introduced into a retrieval system, or transmitted, in
any form, or by any means (electronic, mechanical, photocopying, recording, or
otherwise), without the prior written permission of both the copyright owner and the
above publisher of this book.

The scanning, uploading, and distribution of this book via the Internet or via any other
means without the permission of the publisher is illegal and punishable by law. Please
purchase only authorized electronic editions, and do not participate in or encourage
electronic piracy of copyrighted materials. Your support of the author's rights is
appreciated.

While the author has made every effort to provide accurate telephone numbers and
Internet addresses at the time of publication, neither the publisher nor the author
assumes any responsibility for errors, or for changes that occur after publication. Further,
the publisher does not have any control over and does not assume any responsibility for
author or third-party Web sites or their content.

For Jonny and the three ugly ones

CANDY GIRL

White City

Nobody comes to Minnesota to take their clothes off, at least as far as I know. This ain't no nightclub. Here in the woebegone upper country, Jack Frost is a liberal, rangy sadist with ice crystals in his soul patch. Winter is the stuff of legend: stillborn, snow-choked, still as the ice floes on the ten thousand–odd lakes. The old mill cities are populated by generations of Scandinavian and German Lutherans, rugged souls hewn of blonde wood, good sense and Christlove. The prevailing gestalt is one of wry survivalist humor and thermal underwear with the pins still in the folds. Even the food is properly covered: Everyone's favorite supper is a gluey carbohydrate-rich concoction known simply as "hotdish" and served in community Pyrex. Minnesota is like a church basement with a leaky popcorn ceiling and a bingo caller who's afraid to amp things up past a whisper. A girl who would come to Minnesota to get naked night after night, to hustle for snow-dampened tens and twenties and Benjamins, well . . .

that girl is what a proper Minnesotan euphemistically calls "different."

The strippers here know it, too. *Vegas,* they say. *I need to go to L.A. or Vegas. I could really bank there.* But you sense they're going to stay up north forever, incubating themselves in tanning coffins to create the illusion of sun exposure, frosting their hair.

* * *

In January 2003, when I was twenty-four and punch-drunk on city life, I moved to Minneapolis from my hometown of Chicago. Like many millennial lonely hearts, I had met my boyfriend Jonny on the World Wide Waste of Time (specifically, on a site devoted to the Beach Boys's psychedelic output and Brian Wilson's subsequent foray into radical therapy and pajama drama). Our courtship flowered into existence when Jonny sent me an intriguing e-mail out of the clear blue. Turned out he had possession of a really choice Beach Boys bootleg, a rare instrumental snippet of "I'm In Great Shape" dating from late '66. Only an elite klatch of tight-lipped fat guys had ever been privy to this recording, but Jonny gallantly offered it to me like a sonic gardenia. How could any virgin worth her vinyl resist? I accepted this token of geek love with an (encrypted, virus-protected) swoon, and a romance was hatched. Immediately, I pitched my then-boyfriend to the curb like a spent wad of Bazooka; he was an okay dude, but I had an incurable case of Jonny fever.

Soon, we began sending each other highly confessional mix tapes in padded mailers (nothing says true love like a smoke-colored Sony cassette with handwritten liner notes). Upon request, Jonny sent me photos of himself, his estranged wife neatly excised from each scene with the Photoshop crop tool. I racked up telephone bills that unfurled like the Magna Carta and hit the floor in tandem with my jaw. When a face-to-face meeting seemed imperative, we decided to jet separately to Los Angeles and rendezvous at the Whisky A Go-Go like true rock snobbos. Panicked, I broke out in hives mere moments before our scheduled meeting. Luckily, Jonny disregarded my itchy, eruptive face and stared directly at my tits. We spent the remainder of the day cruising around Hollywood, swilling Corona Extra, and holding hands, our clammy palms epoxied together with flop sweat. It was a first date for the record books, culminating in frantic nudity in a Marina del Rey hotel room. My mother, justifiably freaked by the prospect of my flying cross-country to meet a stranger, had predicted I'd come home in a body bag. But I'd merely bagged a body, and a fine one at that.

Shortly after returning from California, I decided to U-Haul it out of Chicago for good. Obviously, Jonny was sterling, primo, cherry, grade-A boyfriend material. My heart and genitals issued a joint edict that requested I *immediately* relocate to Jonny's home state of Minnesota, and so I soon piloted a moving van across several states, stopping only for a dashboard smorgasbord of sodden fried chicken off I-94. I didn't have much to leave behind in Chicago, save a low-level job at a bankruptcy law firm where a downtrodden woman named Louanne made me file things. My parents were flummoxed by the move, but I had to motor. Love is mysterious and rad, like Steve Perry from Journey.

Once I arrived in the Twin Cities metropolitan area, I moved into Jonny's colonial-style suburban apartment complex, a vanilla variation on the "brick shitbox" school of architecture. The building looked municipal from the outside, like a White House ringer erected on the cheap. Inside our unit, we had white walls, white appliances, white noise and carpets the color of untrammeled sand in Kauai. In Chicago, I'd lived in a cluttered walk-up adjacent to a liquor lounge and a center for homicidal youth. My new lodgings, by contrast, were pin-drop silent. My life felt like a dry-erase board that had been wiped of all its past transgressions and left turns into sordid moral territory. In Minnesota, I could be the most anonymous girl in the world. I could reinvent myself as a lacrosse champ from Topeka if I wanted to. I could feign Mafia ties and carry a teacup Maltese about town. I could change my name to Lynn, get bulimic, and hork ZonePerfect bars into the talking garbage cans at Ridgedale Mall. It was like magic! I had erased myself, just like Lisa Loeb in that one supergay video.

After two days spent wandering shell-shocked around town, I somehow got a job as a copy typist at a Kubrickian advertising agency walled with brushed steel and television monitors. As I filled reams of paper with dopey radio scripts (*void where prohibited*), I watched the snow fall past my twenty-sixth-floor window. The flakes plummeted so swiftly from the gray strata of clouds that they didn't seem to be going up or down. That winter, I dubbed Minneapolis the "White City," because the world around me looked like a blank answer bubble on a standardized test. I didn't know I was destined to make my mark heavy and dark, and that Satan was my exam proctor.

* * *

I liked the ad agency okay. Among the benefits of working there were:

1. A wide selection of regular and decaffeinated teas, including apple spice and orange pekoe.

2. Copywriters on Razor scooters who provided much kindling for my internal scorn furnace.

3. T-1 Internet access, quick like a bunny.

4. Excellent *porn shui*.*

My Internet darling, Jonny, had high hopes for my success in Minneapolis. So I felt kind of bad when I caught some strain of mutant death-flu after only a week in the White City. The virus attacked my legs, and I had to army-crawl from room to room of our sparsely furnished rental. When I finally returned to my new job, I hadn't quite lost my limp. As I hobbled back and forth from my desk to the copier, people stared at me like *Who hired the crip?*

Otherwise, the first weeks at my new home were bright

---

* *Porn Shui*: noun, refers to the art of positioning oneself in one's office or cubicle so that one can surf porn undetected. Usage: "I have great *porn shui*—I face the hallway and the desk behind me is vacant."

and satisfying, as I'd hoped. I'd make kitschy suppers like fondue or shoe-leather pot roast while Jonny (a longtime fixture in the local rock scene) choogled away on his red Epiphone axe. Jonny's three-year-old daughter, a precocious larva with child-star dimples, slept over a few nights a week and seemed initially unfazed by my sudden inclusion in her fissured family unit. When I was home alone, I doggedly tried to finish the heinous novel I'd been writing since college. Inspired by Jonny's musical talents, I tried to learn to play bass guitar, but when I eventually auditioned for a local electropop quintet, the band members looked at me like I was farting the theme from *Mahogany*.

I felt sore about the rejection, and my bass soon acquired a thick patina of dust, which was really crappy, because I had been looking forward to posturing onstage like Kim Gordon or Kim Deal, or any of the assorted lank-haired bassists named Kim who had been my heroines as a teen. I didn't know at that point that I'd wind up "fingering" for an audience countless times in the coming year, though not under the circumstances I'd imagined. (I did peel to Pixies songs on several occasions, so things came full circle, I guess. Thank you, Frank Black, for allowing me to indirectly reference *Un Chien Andalou* in the least intellectual environment ever.)

* * *

In retrospect, I had a pretty life. It was a B+ existence, an eight out of ten (two-tenths deducted for shit weather and death-flu). Still, I felt restless, desperately chasing a buzz like a kid sneaking a nip from Mom's cooking sherry. I was approaching the dark side of my twenties, but I shook like a rattle, still felt like a teenager with fire ants in my Calvins. The big move to Minneapolis had provoked some kind of psychological agita, and I felt like I had been handed a final opportunity to raise some serious heck-ola without facing grown-up consequences. I say "final," because I'd always been a well-behaved human female. Evidence: I'd never ridden on a motorcycle, not even a weak Japanese one. I'd never gotten knocked up or vacuum-aspirated. I'd received every available Catholic sacrament with the exception of matrimony and last rites. I'd completed college in eight tidy semesters (one nervous breakdown per). I'd never thrown a glass of Delirium Tremens in anyone's face. I'd never even five-fingered a lipstick at the Ben Franklin. I was a *drag,* baby. I could feel my wild oats dwindling. My mid-twenties crisis weighted my gut like a cosmic double cheeseburger. I guess that's one reason I ended up half-naked at the Skyway Lounge.

Take It Off

One evening, at the tail end of winter, I was trudging to the bus stop after another numbing day at the agency as a glorified steno bitch. I passed a topless bar tucked away on Hennepin Avenue (even inconspicuous titty bars glare like red rockets) and noted the marquee, which usually read: AMATEUR NIGHT $200 (and sometimes, CITY OF FUN, which I disagreed with). I had a tendency to hurry past the Skyway Lounge as if its molecular aura might give me an incurable case of pubic nits.* But this time, I paused and sniffed the cold air like a hound.

The phrase *amateur night* (relative to stripping) had always conjured a very specific image in my mind: I pictured a knock-kneed drunk staggering down a strip-club

---

* Plus, once when I was in L.A., I passed this club called the Seven Veils, and an extremely foul dude emerged from the shadows. He hissed at me like a cockroach, and I ran away in my stupid, ill-fitting Icelandic sneakers.

catwalk in scuffed bridesmaid's pumps while her husband baits her at the end with a pack of Capri Ultra Lights. *C'mon, baby! I got yer smokes right here! Just a few more feet, Deedee, and we get two hun-derd bigg'uns!* Stripping as a profession sounded super-sparkly, but the idea of undressing on the amateur circuit smacked of cow-town desperation.

Still, I was intrigued. I had only been to a strip club once, in Chicago. It was a somber nude juice bar run by the Russian mob, and I'd felt sorry for the girls somnambulating from table to table, their mouths sewn into half-grins like pretty cadavers. My buddy and I each purchased a lap dance, and exchanged comic stares of titillation and panic while the strippers gyrated passively against our respective groins. My stripper, a shorn androgyne in a latex dress, was an indifferent and inefficient source of heat. When she bent over and spread her buttocks to flash me the ol' Texas red eye, I said, "I like your boots." The experience had been branded on my tender filet o' psyche ever since, and I'd tried to picture myself naked in that crotch-scented hall of mirrors. I couldn't. I was a card-carrying dweeb.

Suppose I were to summon some rare Cody gumption and walk into the Skyway Lounge: Even if I did acquire the guts to strip on a lark, I knew I'd have to answer to a small-but-disapproving female social circle. Most girls I knew hated strippers with the tenor of fury best reserved for serial rapists. They used "stripper" as an adjective to dismiss anything that was crass, blowsy or distasteful. For instance: "Those are stripper shoes, Jen. Get the Maddens instead." Or "Kyle dumped me for some stripper whore who shops at Wet Seal." The average girl in my peer group would sooner have her cuticles pared off with a Daisy razor than allow her significant other to associate with nude girls. This paranoia was bolstered by sensational stories of boyfriends getting their knobs slobbed by strippers in small Minnesota towns like Bemidji and Mille Lacs. It didn't matter if the act was commissioned and paid for; it was entirely the stripper's fault for daring to entertain another girl's hard-won penis. Besides, lots of strippers had breast implants, which was considered treason against womankind, and wildly impractical given the local climate. "Don't they *freeze*?" a friend of mine once wondered aloud. "I can't imagine fishing for pike with my tits full of Slush Puppy."

For whatever reason, I had never felt that bald hostility toward strippers. They were just the dancing ladies of yore, modern-day cantina girls with superhuman breasticles. I'd heard strippers were extremely well compensated for their attentions, so I had trouble believing that they had any genuine interest in purloining someone's else's boyfriend, husband, or Friday fuck. The way I saw it, even the really nasty strippers who gave blow jobs were really just putting in 110 percent at the office. Besides, I secretly imagined all strippers as members of a tight sisterhood who shared hilarious blue jokes backstage, swapped costumes, gargled with Tanqueray and midwifed each other's babies on off nights. There was no way women who paraded naked before men could ever be catty or hateful. They must have cleaved unto one another in their vulnerability; how else would they survive among the dripping mandibles of all those alien men?

Standing outside the Skyway Lounge, I found myself drawn to the bay of blacked-out windows. My heart was banging against my ribs in speed-metal time. I wanted to be in there, part of that spangled corps of women who knew better but walked in anyway. It didn't matter to me that I was somebody's girlfriend or somebody's daughter or somebody's quasi-stepmother, or even somebody's fucking copy typist. I wanted to take shelter in the dank, yeasty darkness, safe from the glare of snow and medium-bright typing paper and the file folders that slashed up the fleshy parts of my palms. I wanted to march into that top-less dive and expose myself to the shadowy goons, winter-ized in parkas and boogeyman balaclavas, who slipped in and out of the door at regular intervals. And so, I respi-rated purposefully several times, and walked in like a first-class dumbass.

* * *

Frankly, I can't read a memoir without a crystalline visual of what the writer looked like at each stage of the narrative. So here you go: A broad walks into a bar, bundled up sen-sibly in winter woolens like any sane resident of a state that borders Canada and dumps frozen precipitation on every exposed head. I was skinny (we neurotics often are), but I had the pallid, pliant flesh of a person who enjoys com-puters and dislikes cardio boxing. My dark hair was cut in a Davy Jones pudding bowl, my nails were chewed to waning moons, and my *maquillage* had sloughed itself off hours ago. I was about 2,000 light-years northeast of Pam Anderson in terms of conventional stripper-chic.

"Hello," I said to the doorman, a fat, grizzled old cuss with the kind of face you expect to see on a titty-bar sentry. He looked like he used to run a boat repair shop until Betty Anne divorced him, and well, you know how that goes.

"What do you want?" he asked me through his graying whiskers. He looked like his kisses would taste like Bac-Os, or the sucked heads of crayfish. Something rank and saline.

"I want to sign up for Amateur Night."

"Oh yeah?" he replied, completely incredulous. This was the first (but definitely not the last) time that someone indicated that I did not look at all like an exotic dancer.

"Yeah," I said with defiance. *Yeah, I wanna get my kit off, fatty!*

Grizzly eyeballed my long patchwork skirt and snow-dredged penny loafers. I looked like a guest lecturer at the Oberlin College Womyn/Transgender Potters' Collective. "You really think *you* can get up there and take your clothes off?"

He gestured to the stage, where a stout Chicana grappled with a brass pole, pivoting to reveal a cesarean scar on her midriff, red as a sockeye salmon. I watched the dancer for a moment and admired her six-inch platform stilettos, solid enough to house a school of betta fish in each transparent sole. Lesson one: Even a birthing-room Betty can be glamorous in the right pair of kicks. I committed this visual to memory.

"Sure," I said. "Obviously. I'm just the type you're looking for."

"Can you show me your body?" Grizzly asked licentiously.

I sighed, shedding the first of many ego boundaries as I parted my long winter coat and revealed my (entirely clothed) body. I was a hippy girl, shaped like a Gretsch bass guitar, but otherwise passable. I didn't have any fresh incisions or Y chromosomes, and my textbook smile bore witness to years of corrective orthodontia in my white, white girlhood.

Grizzly remained dubious. "Can you *show* me?" he repeated emphatically, his man-teats jiggling like silken tofu.

"Like an audition? I don't have anything to wear," I squeaked. Did he expect me to fuck him? I mean, I'd seen lots of porno movies with "audition" scenes. I knew how shit went down, and I wasn't about to mount Lil' Grizzly in some cloistered storeroom.

Grizzly's already-furrowed mug creased like a rubber dime-store mask. He seemed deeply annoyed by my girlish reluctance to disrobe and ride him like a champ. "Yeah, like an audition."

"I don't have a stage outfit with me," I repeated. "I don't own any special clothes. I only wanted to sign up for Amateur Night. It's Thursday, right?"

"Yeah," Grizzly said, resigned. "Just show up."

I left the bar feeling discouraged by the innuendo-spiked exchange with Grizzly but committed to my half-baked, idiotic plan. That night at home, I announced my plan to Jonny while we watched a *Dr. Who* video. He was surprised at the randomness of the idea, but cheered it instantly. Seriously, the boy didn't flinch. You'd think I'd suggested slinging chowder at the local women's shelter, or taking up vinyasa yoga. Not stripping at a topless bar conveniently located less than two blocks from either of our workplaces. I love the guy because he's mellow-yellow to the nth.

"You're going to do amateur night at the Skyway? Honestly, I think it's cool," Jonny said. "You *must* practice in front of me. I've got to see what kind of moves you're planning to bust."

"Too bad you can't actually be there," I said. "It's on Thursday." Jonny's daughter customarily spent the night on Thursdays, and I didn't think my nude public caterwauling should take precedence over his parenting time. That's the kind of "Daddy no-no" that results in biweekly therapy down the road.

"Oh yeah," Jonny said, crestfallen.

"Don't worry about it," I reassured him. "I can do this alone." Frankly, I wanted to go solo. Stripping, though implicitly public, felt oddly private. Also, if I wound up skidding and falling on my can onstage, I didn't want to do it in front of my savory Internet boyfriend.

*   *   *

The next night, I trudged through the congealed sleet to an exotic dancewear emporium in south Minneapolis. Contrary to its image as a city of reeking galoshes, Hüsker Dü T-shirts and snow-caked mittens, Minneapolis is home to at least four shops that cater to its curiously large stripper population. This particular place, owned by an industrious former showgirl, harbored no pretenses of being a lingerie store; it was strictly for working girls of all stripes. I had passed it on my way to Arby's on a couple of occasions, and had peeked in the window at the neatly stacked boxes of Ellie platforms*, display cases of pseudo-Turkish belly chains and salesgays in head-to-toe fishnet. Today, sweating ponds in my peacoat, I deigned to actually enter.

The racks were a riot of fluorescent Lycra, metallic spangles and animal prints; strings, straps and assorted fringe dangled from the costumes like man-o'-war tendrils. A girl in this place could be anything she wanted, from Mackie-era Cher to Cheetara from *Thundercats*. There were bikinis so itsy-bitsy teeny-weeny they occupied negative space. There were exorbitantly priced gowns in black and pink and South Beach tangerine for those who peeled at upscale cabarets and lounges. There were racks of thongs and G-strings to match even the most hideously patterned clubwear. I invented names for some of the more eye-searing ensembles: "Sequined Tigress," "Symphony in Chartreuse and Ochre" and "Shine On, Crazy Rhinestone."

Everything was impossibly small. I sensed my fat ass

---

* A purveyor of shockingly comfortable stripper shoes; I swear Ellies have better arch support than Easy Spirits. I would totally play basketball in Ellies if I didn't have a chronic fear of my glasses getting smashed.

could do more damage to this merchandise than a seam-ripper. The gowns were bad enough, but the fluid poly-ester stripper pants were downright Lilliputian. I swear, I once had a doll named Cricket who wore larger pants than the sizes represented at this shop. Unfortunately, I needed something more than an XXS to cover my slacker fat and lumpen glutes. I was planning to wear a regular black tank and vinyl mini that I already owned, so my stage outfit was already taken care of, however ineptly. But I did purchase a reassuringly thick, grope-resistant black thong, a black feather boa, and a pair of five-inch, clit-pink Lucite plat-form stilettos with sequined uppers. As I paid my $45 and exited the store, I felt like a common whore. It was the best day of my life.

I went back to my apartment, put on Def Leppard's *Hysteria* (a valentine to strippers if there ever was one) and practiced mincing around the apartment. Gait training. I wasn't sure how strippers were ideally supposed to move, so I tried to visualize *Star Search* spokesmodel and Warrant video stunt-cunt Bobbi Brown. In the seminal "Cherry Pie" video, Bobbi swings her drape of platinum hair, purses matte red lips that appear to be plumped with ca-daver fat and catches a falling slice of pie in the Y of her crotch. I lacked the hair, the lips and the magical pie-catching hoo-haw, but I could pout, strut and chicken-flap just like Jagger thanks to years of clandestine practice. A Web site I'd surreptitiously read at work had informed me that strippers were supposed to move slowly, but I was sure guys preferred a manic jeepster on heels to a semi-comatose cold fish. Naively, I assured myself that I knew

what was sexy. Still, I sensed my lifelong lack of coordina-
tion might be difficult to surmount. As I shimmied past
the kitchenette toward the living room, my ankles teetered
on the stratospheric heels, and the deep pile of the carpet
kept pitching me backward. I wondered if I could survive
Amateur Night without shattering my coccyx and spend-
ing the remainder of my career as a typist perched on an
inflatable doughnut.

Ragdoll-for-Hire

Thursday came too quickly; there's a paucity of daylight hours during a long Northern winter and the days run together like the plasmic globs in an egg timer. At work, I typed some unfunny radio spots and guffawed with phony laughter for the sake of the copywriter. I wondered how my coworkers would react if they knew what a bad apple I was, planning to strip for strangers at a low-end place where bus drivers hung out. They'd probably be horrified. The women would snigger into their sleeves like Betty Rubble, and the guys would dismiss me as a maladjusted whore. For the first time in eons, I felt like I still had some cred.

After work, I stopped at home and bagged my stripper accoutrements with shaking hands. I got back downtown too early, and tried to kill time at a chain bookstore crawling with lonely geriatrics and foreign students. My hands shook as I leafed through an issue of *Jane* and drank an ill-advised mocha with whip. Like everything in downtown Minneapolis, the bookstore dimmed and locked its doors at 9:00 P.M., and I was forced to head over to the bar.

Inside the Skyway Lounge, the smoky air was the color of a bad shin bruise. The evening shift was in full swing. A stripper paced the stage in a glow-in-the dark bikini, grimacing at anyone who dared to look away. The whole joint reeked of indifference. I checked in at the front door, and was relieved to see that Grizzly was nowhere to be seen.

"I'm here for Amateur Night," I said to the managerial-type at the coat check. He was the first of many disconcertingly clean-cut young men I'd encounter in the industry. Real suit-and-tie types, the fair-haired sons of the skin trade. I have no idea how these Chipsters wind up working as go-go wranglers. Whatever happened to entry-level positions in copy-machine sales?

"Great," the man-boy replied, handing me a clipboard. (I am now convinced, by the way, that 80 percent of all clipboards manufactured eventually wind up in strip clubs. They're everywhere.) "Write your stage name on the list."

I thought for a moment, then wrote "Bonbon" on the list. I thought I was pretty hilarious.

"Okay, Bonbon, we'll let you know when it's time to get dressed," the man-boy told me. "By the way, feel free to have a drink if you're of age."

Mais bien sûr! I bellied up to the bar, dropped the duffel bag containing my costume and shoes and ordered a

Heinie. As the bartender checked my ID, I noticed a pride of disarmingly childlike strippers drinking soda pop and smoking near the bar. One of them wore cotton scanties and crooked pigtails; she flinched and squeaked as a passing customer honked her breast. It occurred to me suddenly that I would be one of the older girls in the competition, maybe *the* senior contestant in this twisted baby parade. This was a sobering thought. At twenty-four, I'd rarely been the "oldest" in any situation. At the advertising agency, I was practically regarded as a babe-in-arms. Now, here I was, surrounded by Lycra-clad teenagers exhaling mentholated cumulonimbus clouds in the darkness. They stared at my duffel bag with a mixture of hostility and interest; it was obvious that I was not a patron, but a participant in tonight's topless showdown. I nodded at them, then scanned the room for other potential rivals.

There was a blast of icy air, then a girl walked into the bar, hauling a suitcase the size of a bathtub and looking like she'd lost her smile somewhere between Nicollet Mall and Hennepin Avenue. She had limp, ketchup-colored hair, an Easter Bunny face and fucked-up teeth. Weirdly, she was attractive in a foreclosing-on-the-trailer kind of way. She made a show of dragging her bulging valise to a table, then bellied up to the bar.

"Got a smoke?" she asked me.

"I don't smoke," I apologized. "I just drink. Tons."

"I can't drink yet," the girl said, grinning like the "before" photo in a periodontist's office. "I'm only nineteen." She noticed my bag. "Are you here for Amateur Night, too?"

"Yeah," I said, hoping to commiserate with a fellow neophyte. "I'm so nervous. I'm totally freaking out. You?"

"Naah, not me. Been stripping for two years, and I ain't never lost an Amateur Night," the girl said, vermilion gums flashing.

* * *

The stripper onstage, who had now removed her blacklight-sensitive bikini top, began to lob insults at the unresponsive crowd. "I'm fucking *naked*!" she hollered. "You could at least look at me!" A balding man at the tip rail* chortled, and it sounded like a nicotine milk shake.

Soon, a woman with a clipboard appeared at the bottom of a staircase that ostensibly led up to the dressing room. "I need all of the contestants for Amateur Night to come upstairs and get ready," she shouted, arms akimbo.

There were seven of us. We were herded up to a poorly lit room with a low ceiling and the approximate area of a travel-size box of facial tissue. The woman holding the clipboard introduced herself as the "house mom."** A fierce little rubber-band bitch, wearing acid-

---

* *Tip rail*: the seats closest to and/or surrounding the stage. May or may not involve an actual rail.
** *House mom*: a woman employed by a strip club whose job is to resolve disputes, manage the backstage area, apply defibrillator paddles to the bosoms of overdosing strippers and perform other as-needed duties. Usually a former stripper.

wash jeans and a scowl, she somehow looked fifteen and fifty at the same time. She'd lived. The house mom surveyed us briefly, then laid down the ground rules for the competition:

1. No touching the customers during our stage set. (Not that I'd be tempted, since most of the guys in the bar looked stoop-shouldered and scurvy-afflicted, like they lived on Dorals, cheap brandy and Andy Capp's Hot Fries.)

2. No pulling aside our thong to flash the goodies. (Well, pooh. I so wanted to give everyone a *gratis* beaver shot.)

3. No leaning over the tip rail to accept tips. (The conservativeness of this rule surprises me in retrospect, since I later worked at clubs where girls were literally cartwheeling over the tip rail to score that extra greenback.)

Mom then handed out euphemistically named "personnel files," which were blank, brief surveys of our hobbies (crocheting? decoupage?) and favorite sexual positions (Reverse Cowgirl? Hot Karl?). We were supposed to fill them out and hand them to the DJ; he would then share these tantalizing personal details with the crowd while we performed our individual sets.

One of the contestants, a drunk Venus Williams lookalike who called herself Destinee, seemed perplexed by her personnel file. She stared at the questions, half-dressed in a lace teddy, conspicuously menstruating. "I can't read this. Can someone help me fill this out?" she asked, using a wad of one-ply toilet paper to absorb the blood that issued forth like a Mexican flash flood. I read the questions to her, but she wasn't listening. Her eyes were blank and shifty as the viscid blood pooled in her loosely cupped hands. I hastily filled the form out for her with made-up answers. I think I wrote that she wanted to be a concert harpist.

Kayla, the redhead I'd spoken to earlier, was now standing naked in front of the dressing-room mirror, seizing her tiny breasts proudly. She appeared to weigh about sixty-five pounds; both racks of ribs were clearly visible through her translucent flesh. She reminded me of the anatomical glass female at the Museum of Science and Industry in Chicago, whose vascular systems and breast tissue lit up at the touch of a button. "I just had a baby, and see how good I look?" Kayla brayed, clapping her concave belly. The other girls ignored her and slipped into their tired lingerie.

A slippery, gorgeous black girl who gleamed like a chess piece and called herself Mystic boasted about the three grand she'd made stripping in the past week. She eyeballed me coolly as I arranged my feather boa over my shoulders. "You've got a classy look," she declared. "You should be dancing at a sophisticated place, like Schieks. I work there sometimes, and I always mint." I murmured some thanks from within my boa, and got a feather in my mouth.

It occurred to me that I was not in the midst of amateurs. After quickly interrogating the contestants, I discovered that there were only two bona fide amateurs in our motley crew: me, and a trembling Hmong teenager who'd brought at least fifteen friends for moral support. The rest of the contestants were pro-circuit scenesters who worked at other strip clubs in town and had entered the contest anyway for an easy shot at the $200 prize. Well fuck *me*! Uncoordinated, alone and obviously past my prime, I felt doomed.

Still, I was surprised by how undeniably average the girls were. I had always imagined all strippers as sinewy, exquisitely painted Jezebels, airbrushed by genetics and smelling of exotic fragrances like Elizabeth Taylor's "Passion." But there in the sallow light of the dressing room, I saw nails nibbled to the quick, prickly hedgehog vulvae, breasts that hung like worn athletic socks, and bodies of all makes and models, from Ford to Fuck'd. Granted, I was at a working-class strip bar in one of the country's least glamorous states, but still. If these girls could get naked without spooking the clientele, I could certainly strip without fear of being chased offstage by an incensed mob. My confidence scaled up slightly.

* * *

The seven of us handed our personnel files to the DJ (I had filled mine out in haste after completing Destinee's) and headed down the breakneck staircase to the main floor. The dubious contest was about to begin, and the natives were restless, advancing on the hitherto-abandoned tip rail.

It all happened so fast: I went second, after the surprisingly poised Destinee (who appeared to have successfully staunched her bleeding). I inhaled sharply and cantered onstage to "Ragdoll," by Aerosmith. I was concerned about my balance in the pink death-stilts, so I clung to the pole and gyrated like Gypsy. I whipped off my top right away to get it over with. The audience at the rail seemed entertained, in a looking-at-boobs sort of way, and a few of them pushed dollars onto the stage.* As I gamely swung my feather boa over my head, I stared down at my bare tits, almost disbelieving that they were still there. I had half-expected them to disintegrate upon exposure, like vampires pried out of their coffins at high noon.

I shimmied out of my vinyl mini with some difficulty, kicked it to the rail, then strode the length of the catwalk wearing nothing but my Kevlar thong.

"Meet Bonbon!" the DJ boomed over the music. "It says here that her hobbies are PARTYING and GIVING HEAD! Her favorite sexual position is ALL OF THEM!"

I smiled sheepishly at the leering crowd and shrugged as if to say, "What can I tell you? I'm a wayward nympho!" A shabbily dressed man crept up to the tip rail and placed

---

* You know how in the lyrics to "Tangled Up in Blue" Dylan mentions going to a topless bar and staring at a girl's face? He lied. Nobody looks at your face when you're naked—not even nice Jewish boys like Zimmy.

a five-dollar bill onstage. "You should win!" he hissed through his ZZ Top beard.

Newly emboldened by this itinerant fellow's praise, I decided to try a pole trick. I'd seen the veteran strippers doing cool Flying Wallenda-esque moves earlier, and I assumed it couldn't be that difficult. As you may recall, however, one of the Wallendas eventually died in flight. As I tried to wrap one leg around the pole and spin, one of my stiletto heels got caught, the pole wedged in the cleft between the heel and the sole. I spent the next frantic seconds (felt like a year, actually) trying to disentangle myself from the pole while the crowd and the contestants guffawed. *Shazbot!*

I finally managed to free my heel from the pole, and finished my set flushed pink with relief. It felt so bizarre to be standing onstage nearly naked, seeing as I'd always been the kind of girl who fucked in the dark. There was a Jiffy Pop smattering of tepid applause, and I scurried off the stage, shielding my breasts from onlookers as if they were celebrity babies.

The rest of the contest seemed to transpire quickly. I realized as I watched the other girls that I had been hopelessly ignorant about the trends in exotic dance. For one thing, the other contestants reclined on their backs and spread their legs wide enough to impersonate a water-damaged filmstrip about female reproductive organs. This was referred to as "floor work" (a term that seemed unsuitably Olympian for such an unskilled display) and provoked appreciative whistles from the penis gallery.

Also, none of the other girls smiled onstage, opting instead for expressions ranging from Ambien-induced semiconsciousness to searing hate.

The judging was conducted with a disappointing absence of pageantry (I had imagined myself with my arms filled with yawning pink peonies, a rhinestone diadem pinned to my smoky hair). We lined up onstage, and the DJ ordered the crowd to applaud for the girl they wanted to win. (I stepped forward to lame applause, threw a kung-fu kick for a last shot of redemption and still heard the plaintive tweeting of crickets.) The swanlike Hmong girl won handily, since she'd brought a cheering section worthy of a Bruins game. The other girls pouted briefly and marched offstage, hip to the drill. I didn't much care about defeat. I just wanted to put on some clothes and go somewhere that didn't smell bad.

In the dressing room, young Kayla was irate. The girl's mug had gone steam-whistle red, and she stomped her plastic hooves like a horse trained to count. "I've never lost an amateur night," she fumed. "I should'a done more floor work. Normally I wrap my legs around my head and lick my crack. The guys love that. But I ain't got no Vicodin tonight, so I couldn't do it."

"Don't worry. You can lick your crack next time," I said.

* * *

I changed back into my usual uniform of business casual (which someone had unceremoniously scrunched up and hurled into a corner), went outside and hailed a cab. When I returned to the ecru womb of my apartment, Jonny and his daughter were asleep in their respective rooms. I could hear her uneven toddler breathing and his bonesaw-like snores. Girl-specific toys littered the living-room rug, including a naked Barbie orgy that had ended in partial dismemberment. A juice box with the air sucked out of it had been left on the kitchen table, the perfect totem of innocence. I felt shaken, but safe, like I'd fled to an underground bunker after a harsh explosion on Bikini Atoll.

When I was little, I had a detailed world globe that could occupy me for hours when there was nothing on TV. I'd finger the little bas-relief countries and dream of the day when I could travel to places like East Germany, the U.S.S.R., and Beirut, Lebanon (where I mistakenly believed Baby Ruth candy bars were manufactured). The equator was represented by a narrow band of scarlet tape that spanned the circumference of the globe. When I asked my dad about this, he explained that the equator was very hot, and that the closer one lived to the equator, the hotter one could expect to be. As a result, I inferred that everyone who lived directly at the equator was dead, their blistered corpses sizzling like Steak-Umms. How was I supposed to know otherwise? I'd never been anywhere near that ominous red stripe. To me, Carbondale, Illinois, was south.

The Skyway Lounge was kind of like that. I'd never considered the reality behind the black windows, because it hadn't been real to me. Now that I'd been inside and

seen real live girlsgirlsgirls, walking and talking and sur-
viving and smoking Kools, the strip-o-sphere was no
longer as foreign as Brazil (though the two worlds had
pubic-hair trends in common). These girls were living directly on the red stripe, and they were still alive. Still
fierce. I knew I'd be back.

The Ten Best Songs to Strip To

1. Any hip-swiveling R&B fuckjam. This category includes The Greatest Stripping Song of All Time: "Remix to Ignition" by R. Kelly.

2. "Purple Rain" by Prince, but you have to be really theatrical about it. Arch your back like Prince himself is daubing body glitter on your abdomen. Most effective in nearly empty, pathos-ridden juice bars.

3. "Honky Tonk Woman" by the Rolling Stones. Insta-attitude. Makes even the clumsiest troglodyte strut like Anita Pallenberg. (However, the Troggs will make you look like even more of a troglodyte, so avoid if possible.)

4. "Pour Some Sugar on Me" by Def Leppard. The Lep's shouted choruses and relentless programmed drums prove ideal for chicks who can really stomp. (Coincidence: I once saw a stripper who, like Rick Allen, had only one arm.)

5. "Amber" by 311. This fluid stoner anthem is a favorite of midnight tokers at strip joints everywhere. Mellow enough that even the most shitfaced dancer can make it through the song and back to her Graffix bong without breaking a sweat. Pass the Fritos Scoops, dude.

6. "Miserable" by Lit, but mostly because Pamela Anderson is in the video, and she's like Jesus for strippers (blonde, plastic, capable of parlaying a broken nail into a domestic battery charge, damaged liver). Also, you can't go wrong stripping to a song that opens with the line "You make me come."

7. "Back Door Man" by The Doors. Almost too easy. The mere implication that you like it in the ass will thrill the average strip-club patron. Just get on all fours and crawl your way toward the down payment on that condo in Cozumel. (Unless, like most strippers, you'd rather blow your nest egg on tacky pimped-out SUVs and Coach purses.)

8. "Back in Black" by AC/DC. Producer Mutt Lange *wants* you to strip. He does. He told me.

9. "I Touch Myself" by the Divinyls. Strip to this, and that guy at the tip rail with the bitch tits and the shop-teacher glasses will actually believe that he alone has inspired you to masturbate. Take his money, then go masturbate and think about someone else.

10. "Hash Pipe" by Weezer. Sure, it smells of nerd. But River Cuomo is obsessed with Asian chicks and nose candy, and that's just the spirit you want to evoke in a strip club. I recommend busting out your most crunk pole tricks during this one.

Against All Odds

Spoiler alert: During the year following that fateful Amateur Night, a lot of things about me were radically altered. I started to resemble a stripper. I started to move like a stripper, all loosey-goosey and leading with my hips. I earned some serious lettuce. I even learned a few enviably cool pole tricks that could make certain girls black out or thump their melons. But one thing remained the same: I stayed a dork. An outsider. The last kid picked in a gymnasium full of Larry Birds.

When I think of stripping, I'm always reminded of the movie *Almost Famous.* If you haven't seen it (and you absolutely should), it's the story of a teenage journalist named William Miller who tours America with a rock band in 1972. (The story is based on director Cameron Crowe's own experiences as a kid reporter for *Rolling Stone.*) Anyway, William is absorbed into a clique of exquisitely cool people, from the ego-driven band members to jail-bait groupies with names like Polexia and Estrella and

Penny Lane. Even though William is privy to some mad shit on the road, he still retains his essential pie-eyed sweetness (much to his disgust). He wants desperately to be an enigma, to be Brian Jones or Jimmy Page rather than the kid with the notebook.

Stripping, I always felt like a bargain-basement William Miller. I was terminally uncool, surrounded by twisted sisters with fantastic made-up names, wanting to be just as assured and mysterious as they were. Like William, there were moments where I felt at home, like I was born to watch these glittering freaks and hope they threw some light my way. But I never stopped feeling like the kid with three left feet, a millennial icon: the spastic chick.

* * *

True to habit, I didn't tell anyone at work about my one-nighter at the Skyway Lounge. There was nothing to tell, it seemed. I came, I went public with my nipples, I made nine bucks and change in tips. No great shakes, no head-line news. There was a lot of copy to type at the agency, and I didn't have time for revealing small talk about my perverted hobbies. I simply did my job, drained cup after cup of (free!) oolong tea and wrote in my blog during the odd pockets of downtime.

The problem was that I was now obsessed with strip-ping. I had assumed the Amateur Night adventure would slake my thirst for that intangible buzz, but it only made me pant for more. The impossible plastic shoes. The glo-riously imperfect buttocks thunderclapping beneath the strobes. Tan gooseflesh braced against brass. The folded dollar bills made onion-skin fragile from years of club circulation. I wanted to feel the way I had felt onstage again. Agitated. Afraid. More vulnerable than a newborn fawn still mottled with placental muck. If I could have recaptured that feeling by parachuting or finding God or backpacking to Marrakech or *anything*, I would have. But only one thing would hit the glory spot, and that was stripping.

From a logical standpoint, this perplexed me. My night at the Skyway hadn't been particularly fun. In fact, it had been kind of gopher-guts gross. Any glamorous delusions I'd had about stripping had been swept away on the crimson tide of Destinee's menstrual flow. I'd seen dancers being manhandled by customers, their faces twisted with misery (or worse, excruciating expressions of forced pleasure). I'd seen girls mincing from the bar to the stage on grotesquely swollen feet. I'd eavesdropped on the Dickensian hard-luck stories that burbled from the dancers like industrial waste. It was clear to me that real stripping was not all mirth and marabou. You could choke on that lolly if you weren't careful.

However, I knew from watching HBO that not every strip club was the same. Hadn't Mystic declared that I could make money at an upscale cabaret? Hell, I was no Kate Jackson, but I was pretty comely for an egghead. I convinced myself that I'd be a smash on the high-class circuit, the most popular stripper in Minneapolis, sipping Veuve-Clicquot with an amusing Yakuza and pocketing diamonds the size of ostrich eggs. (There would be diamonds, all right. Girls named Diamond, seemingly a new one every week. There were also Rubies, Emeralds and a sapphic Sapphire. No real jewels to speak of, but I had high hopes in the early days.) Yeah, that would be more my scene. I'd get to experience the teeth-grinding adrenaline high of stripping, while still clutching a crumb of dignity to my bosom. It was hip to be a topless entertainer, I reasoned. It was practically *camp*! Best of all, I might make enough money to finally buy the Toyota Corolla I'd dreamed of since childhood.

The Entertainer

I walked to Schieks on my lunch hour several days later. The so-called "premiere showlounge" in Minneapolis was housed in an incongruously stately, historic-looking building. (Pillars, even!) Reading the striped awning above the front steps, I was struck by the hilarity of the name. *Schieks*. On one hand, you had the swarthy, exotic implications of the word *sheik*, but the spelling was pure Minnesota. It sounded like a falafel stand in Duluth. However, Schieks was considered the most upscale topless "cabaret" in the Twin Cities, so I wasn't about to let a lame-ass name dissuade me from inquiring within.

The smell of cigars hit me like a sledgehammer before I even walked through the door. The cigar was *king* at Schieks; it was like the place was run by frustrated tobacconists who had accidentally acquired a strip club. In addition to being displayed open-casket style in the vestibule, cigars were periodically offered as "incentives" with the purchase of lap dances, and most of the patrons mauled cheap stogies while they enjoyed the overpriced lager and overpriced lap-sitters. The stench nauseated me from the first, but I had to get used to it. Everyone eventually did. As long as I didn't end up with a smoldering Camacho in my birth canal, I could cope with middle-class vice.

At first glance, the club was obviously miles ahead of the Skyway Lounge in terms of quasi-Vegas glitz. I walked up to the front desk, which was staffed by a well-dressed, officious teenager, her lips heavily lined with scat-colored pencil.

"May I help you?" she asked.

"Yeah," I said. "Are you hiring at the moment?"

"Waitresses or entertainers?" she asked.

"Uh, entertainers," I said. I was beginning to notice that no one in the industry used the word *stripper,* with the exception of some actual strippers (and even then only the toughest, bitchiest girls). *Exotic dancer* was more popular, and *showgirl* was common parlance at most clubs, though we were a long way from Vegas. Invariably, the official term used by management was *entertainer,* as if we were pulling struggling doves out of our sleeves and telling jokes about Nixon and Passover.

"When can you start?" the girl asked.

"Right away, I guess," I said.

"Fill this out," the girl said, handing me an application attached to a clipboard. "You'll need to come back tomorrow when the manager is here, and she'll go through the hiring paperwork with you. Did you want to start dancing tonight?"

"No," I said, startled. Had I actually been hired? I'd expected a complex and potentially demeaning audition process, complete with nipple-inspection like in *Showgirls.* Instead, they were simply asking me to show up.

"Well, you can work tonight if you change your mind," the girl said, straightening a display of cigars.

* * *

I wandered farther into the club to fill out my application. It was a cavernous, unabashedly opulent space that appeared to have been a ballroom or theater in an earlier incarnation. There were tiered crystal chandeliers, polished brass rails, even a so-called "library" stocked with leather-bound books that I doubted had ever been cracked. The stage was wide and plain, with a mirrored back wall and no pole. Apparently, pole tricks were the domain of downscale titty bars. This was a relief to me, since I was obviously deficient in that area.

I settled into a leatherette throne in the library and filled out the app. When I came to the line for "Current Employer," I scrawled "PLEASE DO NOT CONTACT." I could only imagine the reaction at the agency if they discovered that their copy typist aspired to be a high-priced go-go dancer.

I handed in the application, headed outside and winced at the sunlight glancing off the brackish snowdrifts. The sole feature that Schieks had in common with the Skyway Lounge was the lighting, or lack thereof. Strip clubs are almost always kept dark and at uncomfortably cool temperatures, much like big sexy meat lockers. This ensures that the strippers will look awesome (since any imperfections will be rendered invisible in twenty watts of flickering blacklight) and will be forced to huddle together for warmth (creating the illusion of lesbianism, which managers encourage). Flesh stays taut and cool; private parts remain as fresh and florid as tuna sashimi. All the strip joints in town served their blondes well chilled, though it was hardly necessary during a long winter in the White City.

* * *

When I returned to work and was safely ensconced at my desk, I telephoned Jonny's office. Jonny's workplace was similar to mine: bright, modular furniture, free beverages and lots of hoarse marketing girls with French pedicures.

"Guess what?" I said in a low voice. "I got a job dancing at Schieks."

Jonny was impressed. "They hired you on the spot?" he stage-whispered. "You are so hot! You're ablaze!"

"I don't know," I said. "Nobody even looked at me. Maybe they hire everyone who comes in."

"No way," Jonny said. "They wanted you because you're gorgeous."

I didn't feel gorgeous. I felt like a fatted calf trotting blithely to her own sacrificial bloodletting, but Jonny's words puffed me up nicely. I desperately wanted to be a stripper, but I winced at the thought of inevitable rejection. (Or did I secretly long for the stimulation of ridicule in my otherwise placid life? Deep, man.)

"Are you totally cool with this, baby?" I asked. "I mean, say the word and I won't do it."

"I support you completely," Jonny said. "I don't have an issue with it. I mean, it's just a job. A means of support. It's sexy, actually. Does that make me a pig?"

"Hardly," I said. "I guess I start on Sunday, then."

* * *

That week, I headed back to the stripper store and bought a proper stage ensemble: a short black tube dress and thigh-high fishnet stockings. I imagined myself as a sophisticated vamp straight out of an off-Broadway Fosse tribute, all bobbed hair, cigarettes and attitude. I was sure I'd have to haul my earnings home in a Samsonite. I felt ready. The only thing I lacked was a stage name before I could be a genuine wind-up doll.

I needed something cheeky, yet alluring. The kind of moniker that oozed molten sex, but satisfied my retro fix. I decided on "Roxanne," since that sounded like the kind of girl who lives in a boardinghouse, drinks Pink Squirrels and fucks old men for their gold pocket watches. Easy.

Sunday, I arrived at Schieks ahead of schedule, forever the early bird in an aviary full of night owls. Business hours hadn't begun yet, and the place was vacant but for a few waitresses and bartenders who were prepping for the evening shift. The stage was dark, and I didn't see any "entertainers" on the floor. The place kind of smelled like an old rug that had been latch-hooked with navel lint and cigar butts.

"Hi," I said to an authoritative-looking woman. "Today is my first day of work. Do you know where I'm supposed to go?"

"Oh hi," she said brusquely. "You can start by wiping down the end tables in the VIP area. They can give you a rag at the bar."

I was taken aback. I had to swab the decks in addition to stripping? I figured there had to be a mistake, but I didn't want to balk and sound elitist. Maybe all strippers had to clean. It seemed reasonable, seeing as how they supposedly earned so much. Perhaps the spectacle drew crowds, like a naked maid service.

"Well, shouldn't I change first?" I asked.

"Do you have your uniform?"

"I'm an entertainer," I said. "I didn't know I had to have a uniform."

She looked me over, surprised. "You're an *entertainer?* I'm sorry. I assumed you were a new waitress. Never mind." She chuckled. "The dressing room is upstairs, sweetie." *Hilarious! The pasty wage slave thinks she's a stripper!*

I found a frigid back stairwell and ascended to the dressing room. It reminded me of the girls' bathroom at my Catholic elementary school, with wall-to-wall lockers and a few stiff benches. Not a mirrored vanity in sight; hardly the BaByliss Babylon I'd pictured. Each locker bore a name, and I read them to myself like a misspelled litany: *Tiffanee. Gennifer. Kaitlynne.* I had expected the dressing room to be frothing with feminine chaos, thick with flying undies and claws-out accusations of lipstick theft, but I was utterly alone.

My tube dress fit me like a sausage casing. It rode up

unflatteringly, revealing the hail damage on my meaty hips and creating an unfortunate Esther Williams effect. The stockings squeezed my American thighs accordingly. The three inches of exposed flesh between my hem and my stockings were as pale and malleable as packaged biscuit dough. I put on my stilettos, hoping they'd help, but they didn't. I felt like a *Cathy* comic, only unlike Cathy, I didn't have any methamphetamines to accelerate my metabolism. *Acck!*

Girls began to slink into the dressing room as I applied my makeup with an amateurishly light hand. They wore pastel sweat suits, carried fake Murakami bags and had their expertly foiled hair scraped into Velcro rollers. I expected them to size me up immediately, since I was a suspiciously frumpy stranger, but not one evil eye came to rest on my person. I soon found out that the high turnover at Schieks resulted in the house girls being completely indifferent to new blood. They probably assumed I'd split in a week anyway.

A blonde woman hauling a briefcase and a backpack fiddled with the combination on her locker. She was tan. Really tan. Malignant. She looked like a live reenactment of a dermatologist's cautionary tale; her skin was like umber crepe paper.

"How's it going?" I ventured, since she was the only person nearby.

"Good," she said, undressing. "I haven't seen you here before. Is this your first night?"

"Yeah, it's my first night dancing ever, actually," I said.

"My sympathies," she said, her eyes crinkling. Her face looked around thirty years old, but her breasts were so new I expected to see price tags dangling from the nipples.

"I work at an office during the day, though," I volunteered. For some reason, I was desperate for her to know that I wasn't a dead-end dolly, a subsistence stripper. I had a future. I was salaried and insured, just like Mary Tyler Moore. Stripping was a mere lark, after all. Right?

"Me, too. I'm a realtor," she said. "I just wanted a little extra money."

"Right," I said. "I'm singing the same tune."

"My name is Lisa," she said, extending her hand.

"I'm Roxanne," I said, unsure if I should use my stage name or my real name. It appeared that stage names were the status quo on and off the floor.

Lisa changed into a dress that was identical to mine, only hers was a vulgar pink shade and fit like a custom garment. She wound a garter snugly around her ankle and tucked in a few dollars. Bait, I guess. She looked strangely prim and professional, like she was about to show a split-level Tudor to a prospective buyer or draft an addendum to a purchase agreement.

"Are you going downstairs?" I asked. She was, so I shadowed her like a brain-dead conjoined twin.

* * *

Lisa and I headed down to the main pit. We sat down in an alcove flanked by small curtained-off areas. They reminded me of the dark, crimson-walled confessionals in the Polish Catholic church I'd attended as a kid. "What are those?" I asked. I guessed there wasn't a liver-spotted monsignor waiting behind the curtain.

"Those are the suites," Lisa said.

"The suites?" Do explain.

"Private suites," she explained. "If a guy wants to go into the suite, he has to pay $90 to the stripper and $75 to the club per half hour. Did you buy your suite coupon yet?"

"I have to buy something?" I asked.

"Yeah," Lisa said. "It's a required thing. You pay $20 at the front desk when you show up, and they give you a coupon that waives the club's fee. So your customer can get a private suite with you for only $90."

"That still sounds like a shitload of money for half an hour with a stripper," I observed.

Lisa shrugged. "I guess."

"Can we get our $20 back if we can't convince a guy to use the suite coupon?" I asked.

"No," Lisa said. "But they're pretty easy to sell. Guys like the private suites. I sell my suite coupon almost every night." As she lit a cigarette, her massive breasts bobbled like caramelized flan, and I didn't doubt her success.

"So how does everything else work?" I asked. "Nobody told me anything."

"We give table dances for $20," Lisa explained. "You have to do a minimum of eight table dances a night."

"Is that like a lap dance?" I asked, somewhat alarmed. I hadn't been planning to grind cock, let alone *mandatory* cock.

"Yeah, it's the same thing," Lisa said. "Anyway, once you sell your quota of eight table dances, it comes to $160. At the end of the night, you have to pay out your $160. The management takes $108 of that and gives you back $52. After that initial payout, you get to keep everything you earn."

The system didn't make sense to me. Quotas? Payouts? It sounded like a sales cult. "So, if I earn $160 tonight, they get to keep $108 of that?"

"Right," Lisa said, as if it made perfect sense. "Plus, you should tip the DJ at least $20 per shift."

"Suppose I don't sell eight table dances tonight?" I asked.

"Then you owe them money," Lisa sighed.

"You mean I leave *in the hole*?" I said in disbelief. "What if I sell seven dances, give them $108 and keep my shitty $32? That's their cut anyhow."

"Nope," Lisa said emphatically. "You have to sell eight dances or you owe them." She was complicit with the scam; her blue orbs were blank and blithe.

"Incredible," I said. "I don't see how people agree to it."

"That's how most clubs work," Lisa said. "I mean, if you make $800, that $108 doesn't seem like a lot."

"What's your real name?" I asked suddenly.

"*Lisa,*" she replied, her smile hardening.

* * *

Strippers descended the stairs and filtered onto the floor. The scene was blonde on blonde on blonde; genuine daughters of Norway commingling with peroxided aspirants. Their skin was tanned and oiled to the color of wet cigars. They wore short disco-dolly schmattes, theatrical feather-trimmed peignoirs and long backless gowns slit to Venus. Most were startlingly gorgeous and lean as greyhounds. One of them looked exactly like Gisele Bundchen. Her ass was the size of my goddamned *fist*. I wondered why I hadn't just gotten a night gig at Fuddruckers, since I'd be hard-pressed to earn a Canadian dime amid this kind of competition.

To my horror, I realized that Schieks's cadre of cute waitresses were all outfitted in black minis and fishnet stockings. Crap in a hat! Not only did I already look completely unlike a stripper, but I blended right in with the waitstaff. I imagined I'd be flagged down for more tequila shots than table dances. It dawned on me why the other girls were dressed in either white or shockingly bright colors. As they passed, they glowed like neon tetras in the dark cave of the club. Meanwhile, I vanished into the murk like a plume of squid ink. Invisible.

A small bachelor party had arrived, the first customers of the night. They seemed polite and uneasy as they ordered pints of beer and the requisite cigars. Lisa rose from her seat and blazed toward the men like a Patriot missile. I watched as she sat down among them and engaged them in innocuous conversation. They laughed and stared at her breasts. Her breasts stared at the ceiling. When the next song began, Lisa stood up, peeled off her dress and stood in front of one of the men. The slim brown shoelace of her body undulated between his spread legs. Her gym-toned ass was steeped in body oil. The bachelor's companions smirked and puffed their cigars inexpertly.

A sign in the dressing room had specifically warned that dancers had to remain six inches from the customer during table dances, but Lisa raptly stroked the man's chest and belly with her sculptured nails. She sank to her knees and ran her fingers along his parted thighs, maintaining eye contact for the duration. Her grin was an angry toothpaste commercial, an unyielding Farrah Fawcett grimace. I couldn't stop watching this one-woman Hawaiian Tropic pageant gone wrong. I stared at Lisa's naked back, which was bisected by a single white racing stripe of untanned flesh.

The song ended, and Lisa awkwardly hoisted up her dress. She spoke briefly with one of the men, then turned and gestured for me to join them. I awkwardly rose in my towering heels, and teetered over to join the party.

"The bachelor wants a lap dance from you," Lisa chirped, pointing to the goateed guest of honor. He mutely handed me a twenty-dollar bill.

"I'm not sure what to do, man," I mumbled.

"Just do what I did," Lisa said. "It's easy."

The song began, and if I recall, it was a bumblefuck good-times Shania Twain anthem about beds and boots and cheating. (I should mention that I'm obsessed with Shania Twain, because she's a robot with lifelike vinyl flesh. It was nice to hear her synthetic yodeling during my first-ever lap dance.) I gulped, shoved my dress down to my ankles and began to gyrate against the bachelor.

"Nice!" the bachelor said approvingly. "You've got a great body."

"Thanks," I said. "I'm kind of petrified."

"Oh yeah?" he asked. "Did you just start dancing or something?"

"Tonight," I said. "This is the first lap dance I've ever done."

He chuckled. "Scared much?"

"I told you I was petrified." I stroked the bachelor's cheek like I'd seen Lisa do, then let my hands drift down the front of his flannel shirt. He feigned arousal and closed his eyes like a fat nursing baby. I faintly heard Lisa entertaining the other men with a stupendously dull story about her broken water purifier.

The noxious song ended sooner than I expected; most strip clubs fade songs out at the three-minute mark so lap dances will be teasingly brief. The motivation for this tactic is more prurient than prudish; the more songs it takes for a man to cream his Dockers, the more cash the girls pull in.

"Thanks," I said, wriggling back into my dress.

"You've got nice hips. You remind me of Shakira," the bachelor remarked.

"Somewhere in Colombia, Shakira bristles at the comparison," I replied.

* * *

The club had begun to fill with nondescript men. The stage rotation had begun, and I realized that I hadn't notified the DJ of my existence. There was only one stage at

Schieks, and girls took turns performing two songs at a time. As I made my way backstage, a man asked me if I could bring him another Sam Adams. "I'm not a waitress," I replied politely. Why in the name of Lucifer had I opted to wear arid, boring black in a veritable gulf of iridescent, wet-look cheetah prints?

The backstage area was underwhelming and unfurnished but for a mirror. There were a few girls hanging out back there, but it was mainly used as a passage on and off the stage. A topless girl who had just completed her set stood next to the DJ booth, chatting with him nonchalantly. She wore an Egyptian death mask of makeup and a fake ponytail so long it twitched against her rump.

"I haven't taken a shit in a week," she fretted. "I'm starting to get worried."

"Have you tried bran cereal?" the DJ asked. "Canned pumpkin?"

I approached the booth timidly. "Hey. I'm Roxanne."

"Nice to meet you, Roxanne," the DJ said, scribbling my name on his notepad. The list wasn't very long, and my stomach reared with the realization that I'd be onstage sooner than I realized. "What kind of music do you dance to?" the DJ asked.

"Hair metal," I said stubbornly. It had become obvious to me that most girls favored lascivious R&B tracks, but I wanted to kick it old-school. Like the tongue-waggling video sluts I'd idolized as a kid. Like Tawny Kitaen dry-humping the car in that Whitesnake video, or that girl from *Cheers* who wore the "Raspberry Beret."

"Sure," he said. He switched on the mic and transitioned from his normal voice to his incredibly unctuous DJ voice: "LET'S KEEP THE PARTY GOIN'! Here COMES TAAAAAAAAY-LOR!" On cue, Taylor appeared, brushed past us, pushed open the mirrored stage doors and threw herself to the wolves.

"Dude, that voice is *sick*," I commented once he'd turned the mic off again. "How can you stand hearing yourself like that?"

"This is a good job," the DJ said, shrugging.

* * *

Soon enough, it was my turn to keep the party going. As I stepped onstage to "Armageddon It" by Def Leppard, I realized Schieks wasn't hosting much of a bash. The customers looked bored and flaccid, more interested in the Vikings game on TV than in the half-naked dolls who were curled in their laps. The strippers who weren't with customers were sulking near the bar, smoking so aggressively that I imagined their young lungs looked like blackened lamb chops. Out there, it was joyless and airless.

Onstage? It was sublime.

Joe Elliot sang the body electric. Phil Collen strummed my pain with his fingers. My heart thumped against my ribs as I pulled off my dress and spun to face the back of the stage. In the mirrors, I saw myself standing topless before a backdrop of faces. It was so cold in the room that my nipples shrank to pinpricks and my legs were covered with gooseflesh. I didn't give a fuck. I was on fire.

I pranced to the center of the stage like Mick Jagger on

Hullabaloo, throwing a few rock kicks for effect. I noticed some of the strippers in the back were whispering to each other as they watched me, and I knew it was because I danced like a tool. It was the only way I knew how to dance. I've always been graceless and hyper, so it was only natural that I danced that way. If I wanted to be a languid Salome, I'd need a fistful of disco biscuits, and downers are hard to find in strip clubs.

The second song began, and I was running out of ideas. "Floor work" was strictly forbidden at Schieks, and as I mentioned before, there wasn't a pole or a tip rail. Strippers were basically limited to pacing the stage and posing like models. It seemed like a disservice to Def Leppard to be so banal, though, so I tried to really pump up the jam. I skipped from one side of the stage to the other, spanked my ass insouciantly and twirled around to the seismic thud of the one-armed drummer.

"Say good-bye to beautiful Roxanne!" the DJ boomed. I waved to no one in particular, grabbed my dress and scurried offstage.

(Strange that I always use the word *scurried* to describe how I exited the stage after a set. That's exactly what I did, too. Everyone scurries when they're starting out. It's a natural response to the jarring realization that one is naked in public. I know that doesn't make sense, since strippers are used to being naked, but something about the end of a stage set produces a primal feeling of vulnerability.)

With my stage set over, I knew I had to hustle for lap dances. It was a weird series of maneuvers: sit with customer, engage in awkward badinage while batting the lashes at hummingbird speed, ask him if he wants a lap dance, repeat, persist, sparkle. For every "yes," there were at least fifteen rejections. Over the course of the next few hours, I managed to stiffly administer a few lap dances, but there was plenty of downtime for gawking at the other strippers. Fascinating stuff.

They cruised the room like thin, tawny cats, their legs like jointed drinking straws, their protuberant breasts leading the parade. They had no physical boundaries. Unsolicited, they climbed onto customer's laps. They languidly picked off of fruit plates and appetizer samplers. They buried their heads against dudes' peckers, miming fellatio. They led a succession of suckers into the private suites (to actually suck them off? I wondered). Some of them canoodled with the same men all night, whispering hot nonsense in their ears, stroking them off beneath the linen-covered tables. They were better than girlfriends; they were fabulous fakes. I couldn't fathom how they did it so convincingly, wooing those graying Lutheran husbands like long-lost sweethearts. I couldn't follow suit.

The scene on the stage wasn't nearly as interesting as the psychosexual drama unfolding on the floor. Most of the girls looked bored during their sets and moved like poorly articulated action figures. They danced mostly to nondescript dance beats and shrugged off their clothing nonchalantly. Although the customers watched intermittently from their tables, the colored lights glancing off their bald pates and aviator lenses, they never approached the stage to tip. I thought that was strange, especially since Schieks's clientele were known for being rich white-collar types with *dinero* to spare-o. The Skyway might have been a dive by comparison, but the tough dames there had been a lot more fun to watch.

After unsuccessfully trolling the "library" for customers, I decided to return to the dressing room to count my money (Kenny Rogers would disapprove, as my dealin' was far from done). I'd lost track of how much I'd earned, and there was a sizable stack of twenties tucked in the vinyl top of my stocking. However, as I walked toward the staircase, my stocking slipped and my wad of ill-gotten gains fell to the floor.

"You need to get a garter. You're going to lose all your money that way," a passing stripper scolded as I bent to recover my earnings. She showed me how she wrapped her garter around her ankle and twisted the bills a special way to secure them. I thanked her, and continued toward the dressing room.

As I took the stairs, an apple-cheeked Katie Holmes doppelgänger nearly knocked me over, clapping a few shreds of white lace to her body. An ardent customer had torn off her lingerie. She hooted with laughter at my startled expression. "Welcome to Schieks!" she yelled, thundering up the dressing room stairs like a ghost in tatters.

The shift was over more quickly than I expected. Like every stripper every night, I wanted just a few more hours, a couple more chances to find the perfect mark and rob him blind. I hadn't sold my "suite coupon" (the private suites spooked me, frankly), and I hadn't earned much over my quota. As I paid out the house at the end of the night (a chilly ritual that seemed to assign a price to my very head), I realized that I was ready to crash. Being an entertainer at Schieks was harder work than I had anticipated, kind of like being a Fuller Brush man in fetish heels. A two-song set at the Skyway hadn't prepared me for the reality of the Scheiks hustle. My three exhilarating stage sets had been worth it, though. *Hullo, Minneapolis! We are Roxanne!*

When I came home, I took the money out of my wallet and rifled through it intently, as if each bill were a mysterious document. Then I took a scalding hot shower before crawling into bed with Jonny. I scrubbed my thighs and belly like Meryl Streep in *Silkwood* and thought about how repulsive stripping was, how cold. Could there be anything grosser than pleading with undesirable men for three minutes of their company? The whole ritual defied logic, nature and the time-honored tradition of "Schlub Chases Babe." I wondered if the customers ever spotted the naked disgust behind the mirage of inviting smiles. But I knew I'd go back there. Continue the charade. Learn to bank.

* * *

The next morning at the agency, I felt wrung out. I'd worked until 1:00 A.M. at Schieks, and my feet looked puffy and irregular, like swollen pink Floridas. Still, I'd taken home almost $150 in mangled bills, and that was no chump change to a copy typist. I decided that this stripping gig would be worth keeping, if only for a couple of nights a week. I could increase my earning potential, as they say in the scam rags. I wasn't one for being phony, but

it wouldn't hurt to get a better outfit (brightest chartreuse), maybe quit gnawing my nails bloody and go on
one of those fad diets that recommend steak and whipped
dessert topping for maximum weight loss.

It wasn't enough to be a nude girl, I decided. You had
to be *the* nude girl. You had to sparkle, you had to corus-
cate, you had to bounce like the phantom cheerleader in
the vault of every man's memory. Your skin had to be
oiled to reflect the purple strobes, your hair had to
be coaxed into a voluminous Nashville tangle. You had
to possess the vein and make the puppet rise. You had to
make the average man's wife look like one of van Gogh's
potato-noshing peasants by comparison. Coarse. Earthy.
Plain. It was, I realized, a tall order.

* * *

Later that night, Jonny and I shared cocktails and schemes
at our haunt-of-choice, a cozy bowling alley called the
Texa-Tonka where Jäger-pounding jocks peacefully coex-
isted with local eccentrics.

"I could have done better," I confessed. "I mean, I saw
girls who were going home with ten times the money I
made."

"It was your first night," Jonny reasoned, nursing the
dregs of a dirty vodka martini. "You can't expect to make a
thousand dollars right away."

"I looked all wrong," I said. "The other girls were
pornographic. I always thought I was kind of cute, but I
must have been kidding myself."

"I've got to come in and watch you work," Jonny insisted. "I bet you're spectacular. You've got something special that they don't have. You're rock 'n' roll, man. You're tops!"

"Darling," I sighed, employing my favorite term of endearment for the boy. "You'll be the ruin of me."

I knew how lucky I was to have a guy like him. He made me feel like my whole ass-for-hire scheme was clean, sexy fun. I needed his levity in order to continue, because the reality of Schieks was like being locked in a humidor with a thousand grasping zombies. Jonny's idealism fueled my one-woman muscle car, made we want to keep mowing down the undead and raiding their wallets. *Vroom,* baby.

Parallel Lines

I began working on Sundays and Wednesdays, from 7:00 P.M. until closing time. In an attempt to compete with the savage babes at Schieks, I bought two new outfits: a sparkling dress of wide-wale mesh that had an unfortunate tendency to snag my nipple piercings, and a pale pink halter dress that I immediately retired when I encountered a girl of sumptuous proportions wearing the same item. (The black tube dress wound up exiled to the darkest perimeter of my closet, where my cats discovered it and promptly christened it with piss.)

Mysteriously, I was advancing at the agency. My boss had taken a shine to me and was hinting at a promotion. I needed the money, but the idea of increased responsibility made me quake in my Chuck Taylors. There was a simplicity to being a typist that I relished. Copywriters cruised over to my desk on silver Razor scooters and dropped off the revisions they'd made to their scripts. I updated the copy, printed it and sent it through a gauntlet of grim proofreaders. I was a genial robot in Old Navy career wear, quick with a quip and able to lavish even the most uninspired frozen-food advertisement with heaps of insincere praise. This translated to mild popularity in the serpentine corridors of the agency. I didn't want to upset the ecosystem with a promotion.

I was aware that my coworkers could come into Schieks and see me shaking my moneymaker, but it seemed unlikely. The people at the agency were too self-consciously hip to go to a titty bar (they generally favored Nye's, a Polish restaurant with live polka music and geriatric regulars, for their weekly exercise in condescension). I didn't sweat getting caught with my pants down, so to speak, because I was confident that none of my *au courant* agency peers would bother showing up at an airless morgue like Schieks. The place was so anti-cool.

You sense where this is going, right? My third time working at Schieks, two of my coworkers showed up. I didn't know them very well, but I recognized them as roving troubleshooters from the IT department. Nerds! I caught them staring at me, slack-jawed, as they settled in at a table near the stage. Confusingly, I felt a surge of slumber-party giddiness when I first spotted them. It was almost as if I'd been secretly hoping to get caught, though the prospect horrified me on a conscious level.

That night, I was wearing my new mesh outfit and doing miserably. "I don't like the dress," a patron told me flatly as he bounced me on his knee. (I'd learned to deep-six my phobia of cooties and cuddle with the bastards.)

"Well, what do you like?" I asked seductively, hoping he'd ask me to lose the dress entirely.

"Really small blondes," he replied. "Like her." He pointed to one of several girls named Diamond who worked at Schieks during my tenure. This one was a Kate Hudson look-alike with cherubic curls and a gamine body.

"Hey, Diamond," I called out.

She pivoted and stared at me.

"I think this dude wants a dance from you," I said, climbing off his lap.

Diamond weaved through the crowd, a rhinestone *Playboy* bunny pendant winking against her xiphoid process. She always looked very warm, even when the temperature in the meat locker was intolerably low. Not just warm in the basic physiological sense, but warmed *up*, like a horse that had been exercised for hours, all pliant flanks and clean sweat. The best strippers have this quality, and Diamond was definitely a blue-ribbon show pony.

"Hi," Diamond said to the guy, eyeing me warily. It was more than unusual for a stripper to relinquish her customer to another girl, but what was I supposed to do? Hound the dude for action when I wasn't his preferred flavor? I was too proud for that shit. I still wanted to believe in the cult of stripper-worship, even if it was a charade. If a gal zeroed in on the right customer, she would be treated like a deity (and paid in kind) until the lights went up. Begging, extortion and/or haranguing a reluctant guy into parting with his cash? Not quite so appealing. I wanted the guys to savor the attention I granted and return it in kind. If they didn't? Send in the blonde.

As Diamond attended to her new pal, I found myself impulsively walking toward the table where my two workplace acquaintances sat and gawked at the entertainment. There was a sinewy Russian girl onstage, a trained ballerina who whirled in reckless circles as though the grand prize for effort was a Baptist's severed head.

"Hi," I said. "Care if I join you?" I figured their money was as good as anyone else's. Besides, they'd already spotted me.

"Not at all," one of the IT guys said. As I sat down, we were immediately dive-bombed by a cocktail waitress. Schieks trained them to descend like carrion birds in fishnet hose and pressure the customers to buy cocktails for the strippers. I ordered a vodka Red Bull: upper meets downer in an effervescent hybrid of bubble gum and junkie piss.

"So, where do you work?" Computer Guy No. 1 asked.

"I work at an advertising agency," I said, daring him back.

"So do we," interjected Computer Guy No. 2. "Which one do you work at?"

I told them. They glanced at each other, their faces crumpling in pained smirks. The jig was up. I was officially grist for the office gossip mill.

"You work there, too, don't you?" I asked. I sensed that they were more embarrassed than I was, since their faces had gone cerise.

"Yeah," No. 1 said sheepishly. "We *thought* we recognized you!"

"This is my night job," I said. "The agency pays shit, as I'm sure you're aware."

"Oh yeah," No. 2 said, relaxing a bit. "Totally."

"Don't tell anyone," I said, cocking an eyebrow. I have remarkable eyebrows. Everybody has their something, even grade-D strippers.

"We won't tell on you if you don't tell anyone we were here," No. 1 offered.

"That sounds like a fair trade," I said, inhaling my caffeinated booze through a dinky bar straw. Actually, it didn't, but I was grateful for the proposal. I had a lot more to lose if I was outed at work, whereas no one would penalize two red-blooded network administrators for going to a strip club.

"How long have you been dancing?" No. 2 asked cautiously.

"I just started last week," I confessed. I disliked the question. It had a way of instantly dissolving my patina of cool and exposed me as the quaking newbie I was. I envied the girls who'd been stripping for years, even though they all had hammertoes, coke-worn sinuses and intimacy disorders as a result. They were *cool.* They had champagne in their veins; they glowed like radium. Customers bought them appetizers, jewelry and the occasional Porsche.

"Do you like it?" they asked.

"Sure, it's awesome," I said.

We sat in pensive silence for a few moments. I ordered another vodka Red Bull, since the first one hadn't done much to loosen the stubborn knot in my stomach.

"So," No. 1 finally said. "How about a dance?"

"Seriously?" I said. "You want a dance from me?"

He nodded. I wondered how long they had been drinking.

The DJ cranked "My Sharona," and I shimmied out of my mesh dress. No. 1 leaned back, parted his legs and placed his hands at his sides, the universal posture of lap-dance recipients.

"I'd better get my hardware upgraded for this," I joked as I kneeled between his legs and gingerly stroked his thighs.

"Sure," No. 1 said, his eyes half-closed. "Whatever you want."

I shoved my cleavage in his face and gently buffeted his cheeks with my tits. "That's nice," he said approvingly.

"Maybe you can bill this night of debauch to the agency," I said. "Tell them we were having an important status meeting."

He laughed. "I wish."

* * *

Hours passed, and I had performed at least five lap dances between the two computer guys. I had ridden more nerd jock than a hooker at an electronics convention. Meanwhile, the boys grew increasingly polluted on Schieks's finest imported beer offerings.

"I've had a crush on you for weeks," No. 2 slurred. "Whenever I see you in the elevator at work, I want to talk to you, but I'm real scared."

"Right," I said, counting my bills briskly. "I think

that's the Guinness talking. Yeah, it is. I distinctly heard a brogue."

"No, seriously," he insisted, handing me another twenty-dollar bill to disrobe yet again. "You are *sooo* beautiful."

"Man, you are going to be so embarrassed the next time you run into me at work," I said. "In fact, I'm going to be pretty squicked myself."

"No," he insisted. "It's all good. I won't be embarrassed."

I finished the last dance, excused myself and ran up to the dressing room. The situation had acquired a certain gravity, and it was freaking my scene. Still, I had about thirty ounces of well vodka effervescing in my bladder. (I rarely boozed at work, even though most of the girls I worked with couldn't bring themselves to solicit a single lap dance without a few shots of liquid hubris beforehand. They smoked joints and downed budget champagne in the stairwell, and the potent combination of ganja and swill made them walk pigeon-toed.) I flopped down dizzily on a bench and counted out my green: three hundred bucks. Not bad for a frosty Wednesday night in the city that never wakes.

The next time I passed the computer guys in the hallway at the agency (and ever after), they couldn't bring themselves to look at me or offer a greeting. I'd anticipated that reaction, but it was still unexpectedly sad.

Material Girls

After several weeks of working at Schieks, I decided that strippers were the most fascinating, inscrutable animals I'd ever observed. On a busy night, there could be fifty girls working the room in various states of undress (and sobriety). While this made for an endless rotation and limited my stage sets to only two or three per night, I relished the chaos. Schieks was a fulgent, slow-motion bacchanal of disembodied breasts, tipped champagne flutes, Coco Red lipstick and invisible math. *Four more dances,* girls murmured to each other in private moments. *Two more dances and I'll make house fee. Ten more and I'll make rent.* They changed costumes frequently, superstitiously, as if wearing a different fluorescent color would dramatically redirect the evening's cash flow in their favor. *This is my money dress. I always make money in this dress. Just watch.*

I never changed my costume during a shift. I figured the customers weren't there for a fashion show. They went home and crept into the marital bed and masturbated to the afterimage of a certain pair of tits, a particular ass, the costly touch of a paraffin-soft hand. They didn't care if their mental fuck was wearing a red gown or a gold one. But the other girls were insistent that the opposite was true. They claimed that men were such slaves to visual cues that the right color or fabric could mean the difference between a $500 night and a $1,000 night. Maybe they were right. Sometimes the theory was bolstered when a girl changed clothes and immediately banked, but usually, the evidence was inconclusive.

There was one inviolate principle that even I came to recognize: Men dig white shoes. A girl invariably made more money when she wore shining white stripper-stilts instead of black. White shoes evoke summertime, innocence, the ruddy-chested ICU nurse bearing post-tonsillectomy marshmallow sundaes, the girl on the pier in seersucker shorts who remained 99.44% pure until college, new roller skates. Good girls wear white. Men respond in kind. A tan girl in white shoes was irresistible; unfortunately, I was pale enough that white shoes blended seamlessly with my flesh.

Of course, the strippers also took pains not to appear too innocent, valorous or bookishly inclined. (In direct opposition to the Swayze Mandate of 1987, everyone puts Baby in the goddamn corner.) The ideal persona to assume on the floor was that of a self-centered, brain-dead circus contortionist, loose of both moral and sinew. This was a difficult exercise in mixology, but a successful actress could retire in furs by twenty-eight and buy a four bedroom Tudor in Shakopee.

You couldn't miss the garter of a girl who had banked. The carefully pleated money sprang out every which way in a garish green starburst. This odd flower was worn with pride, like an ankle corsage at a topless prom. The strippers at Schieks never carried purses; they wore their money against their bodies and in full view. Like a Girl Scout merit badge, or a retroactive price tag, this display of cash ensured that everyone was aware of everyone else's price per pound. Sometimes a girl who had a devoted regular customer carried thousands of dollars strapped against her delicate tibia, a practice that was risky but looked totally cool.

Regulars, or "regs," are the bread and butter of upscale strip clubs. A reg spends inconceivable sums of money on one cherished girl, and at Schieks, the regs appeared with, well, regularity. One stripper, Sidnee, had a reg who came to see her at least three times a week and handed hundred-dollar bills to her as if they were pocket lint. Sidnee rarely danced onstage (she was too busy attending to her smitten reg), but when she did, she always peeled off her lingerie to an urgent techno song called "I Need a Miracle." It seemed fitting, even though some would argue that Sidnee needed a miracle less than any of us. Her reg kept her rich. But I knew that her standard of living was contingent on the interest of one middle-aged man in a Cosby sweater. If his obsession ever waned, she'd be back to steerage with the rest of us, hawking two-for-one laps with a free cigar-cutter included.

Once in a while, a customer of mine promised to return to Schieks specifically to see me. "What nights do you

work?" they'd ask. I feigned delight at their interest, but I
knew they probably wouldn't come back. I never offered
enough of an incentive. Sex with a customer was out of the
question, and I didn't even pretend to consider it. And it
was about sex, always. Fucking was the natural endpoint of
the stripper-reg relationship, and it was also the quickest
route to a new car or a sapphire bracelet to hock. I wouldn't
fuck anyone for money, though—and not just because of
Jonny, who was mysteriously comfortable with the idea of
pay-for-play—but because the idea of physical reciprocity
in that context revolted me. I had no problem grinding on
customers, touching them or even granting the occasional
coquettish kiss on the cheek if I thought the gamble might
pay off. But the idea of one of them freely touching me in
return was nauseating. A mouth on my tit, a hand on my
ass? Gag me with the keys to a Karmann Ghia.

I'm not sure when the money began to matter to me. I
had come to Schieks mainly for kicks, to be the kind of
wanton slutburger Magdalene who had been vilified in the
churches of my youth. I had also come because I was sub-
consciously rejecting the grown-up position I was being
nudged into by my boss. Being accountable for other people's profits terrified me more than the sex industry ever
could, and I sensed the need to escape the rabbit warren
of gainful employment before they got me for good. For
the first time, I was seeing the alternative: living by my
wits, pissing on my solid Second Wave feminist education,
becoming a con artist disguised as dimbulb arm candy.
And I *liked* it. Plus, Schieks's payout structure forced me to
crave cash; if I didn't make their money back first, I'd

never make any for myself. It turned us all into buzzards, circling the room even after every customer had been picked over. We needed to justify the indignity of wearing thongs in public. We needed to bank.

To my surprise, we were required to sell more than lap dances. Entertainers at Schieks also had to circle the room periodically with T-shirts, caps, cigars and manicure kits, offering them to customers at a "discount price" with the purchase of a dance. I didn't particularly mind this until I was informed that we were heavily fined for the items we failed to sell. Not only did the merchandise sales bring the already-competitive atmosphere to a fever pitch, but the constant shilling embarrassed everyone. It's tough to maintain one's erotic mystique while trying to pressure a guy to buy a $40 pair of nail scissors. Whatever happened to just getting naked? The corporate bullshit made me long for the relative purity of the Skyway Lounge. (They kept it real at the Skyway, man!)

Sometimes, though, the money traveled fluidly from a customer's billfold into my silver garter. On these nights, I felt bulletproof and diamond-hard. I'd arch my back over a guy's pelvis during a lap dance, caress my bare breasts and stare up at the gargantuan crystal chandelier. It was cinematic, decadent, almost absurd to see myself reflected that way in the mirrored ceiling panels. I would have barely recognized the girl who stared back at me if it hadn't been for the tattoos.* Her eyes were so passive, so assured. She had mastery over her body, something I'd

---

* Incidentally, my tattoos are totally bitchin'.

never been able to claim. I'd always been clumsy and wary of my body's limitations. As a kid, I hadn't even been able to control my bladder, let alone my limbs. But this girl, my mirror image, didn't know anything about that. Stripping had stolen her memory, stripped her membranes and made her into a new animal.

Sexy bitch, I'd mouth at my reflection. Those were the good nights. But there weren't enough good nights in the naked library. Not for me.

I knew I would never find the money I suddenly desired if I stayed at Schieks. I was too unconventional-looking and not nearly companionate enough to slake the aging vampires who frequented the club. But instead of quitting stripping for good (like I had originally planned to do after a couple of months) I researched alternative clubs. I found my answer in Minneapolis's warehouse district, in a three-story building the color of strawberry sherbet. Welcome to Big Pink.

Big Pink

After a particularly bad week at Schieks, I made a firm decision to score a gig stripping elsewhere. I decided on Deja Vu, a large franchise club affiliated with *Hustler* magazine. The Vu was the most notorious club in town, and I'd seen many seasoned girls wrinkle their noses in distaste at the mere mention of the place. It was a wild joint, they claimed. A "hustle club."* It was the antithesis of Schieks's genteel, slow-motion approach to adult entertainment. Plus, the dancers were fully nude at Deja Vu and lap dances there were rumored to be far more risqué. It wouldn't seem like an obvious first choice for a new workplace.

However, one day at Schieks, I was talking to Tammi, a chesty, sad-eyed blonde who always shocked me with her

---

* *Hustle club*: noun, a strip club where girls use an impersonal, hard-sell approach, moving quickly from customer to customer rather than flirting at length or feigning an intimate connection.

mundane anecdotes about yard work and property taxes.
"I'm just not making any money here," I told her. "I hate
sitting with the guys for hours and pretending to be interested in racquetball and tech stocks."

"You should go to Deja Vu," she rasped. "If you like to
keep moving, it might be more your scene."

The next afternoon, Jonny and I walked through the
muddy spring snow to Deja Vu. I'd never laid eyes on the
pink brick building before, and I was overwhelmed by its
size. It was the biggest strip club in the area, featuring
three floors of entertainment. An awning above the door
advertised 1000'S OF BEAUTIFUL GIRLS AND 3 UGLY ONES.
I shuddered as we ducked inside.

The club looked nothing like Schieks and exactly like
every strip club I'd ever seen in the movies. It was lush
wall-to-wall sleaze, all dark velour, bordello styling and
bad hotel-lobby carpeting. The main stage was ringed by a
tip rail that could accommodate at least twenty. Above the
stage was a glass-floored second stage, which allowed customers to look up and watch another girl dancing overhead. This multidimensional display of poontang
reminded me of the 3-D chessboard on *Star Trek*, which in
turn reminded me that I was a huge nerd.

A two-story pole connected the second stage to the
first stage, allowing daredevil girls to slide down like fire-
fighters and begin their stage sets on a dramatic note.
There was a nonalcoholic bar against one wall, where customers purchased their mandatory $9 soft drinks upon
entering. (Most fully nude clubs in Minnesota don't have
liquor licenses.) I snickered at a banner advertising

O'Doul's nonalcoholic beer. Imaginary suds struck me as a very appropriate strip club beverage. Illusory intoxication, the name of the game.

Jonny and I paused to watch the stripper on the main stage from a distance. "This place is balls," I muttered.

"That girl is dancing to Kiss!" Jonny remarked admiringly. The dancer scaled the pole, climbing effortlessly to the very top. She flipped upside down and unhooked her bra, dropping it to the stage below. She pulled herself back upright, then swung her legs over head in an aerial split. She was like the Olga Korbut of adult entertainment.

"And she's getting tips," I pointed out. "Look." The men seated at the tip rail withdrew their wallets in succession and dutifully placed dollars on the stage. This thrilled me, as girls were rarely tipped onstage at Schieks.

I flagged down the manager (whom I identified by the requisite clipboard he carried). All the night managers at Deja Vu looked the same to me: mustache, gleaming dark hair, monkey suit. Even after several months of working there, I still had difficulty telling them apart.

"Hi," I said. "I'm interested in working here."

"Okay," Mustache said brusquely. "Let me find a girl to show you around." Before I could open my mouth to ask another question, he ducked backstage and returned with a tan, gum-snapping girl in a Day-Glo bikini.

"This is Sherry," he told me. "I told her to give you a tour of the club."

"I've been at this place forever," Sherry informed me.

"Okay," I said, helplessly waving good-bye to Jonny.

* * *

Sherry took me up to the third-floor dressing room in a rattling death trap of an elevator. She had fake breasts the size of muskmelons, but other than that, she looked nothing like a Schieks girl. She was healthy. Cheap. She looked like she'd spent the day roller-skating at the beach, then accidentally pitched face-first into a vat of Bonne Belle warpaint.

"So, have you danced before?" she asked me in a thick Minnesota accent.

"Yeah, at Schieks," I said.

"They're robbers, them guys," Sherry commented.

"Tell me about it," I said. "That's part of the reason I'm leaving. So how much do you pay the house here, then?"

"They count your lap dances," Sherry explained. "At the end of the night, you have to pay a $20 shift fee, plus $7 for every $20 dance you get."

I did some quick mental math. "So, if I get ten dances, or $200, I have to give the club $90 of that? That's a lot of money."

"Yeah, but you get to keep all your stage tips," Sherry said. "And since they only charge you for the dances you actually get, you'll never owe the house more than you've made."

"That sounds reasonable," I said, even though it didn't. Still, it was an improvement on my current situation. I actually owed Schieks $50 and counting in back house fees.

The dressing room at Deja Vu was a tiled labyrinth vibrating with stripper activity. I was fascinated by the lockers, which were plastered with glittery bumper stickers, Polaroids, political statements and personal vendettas scrawled in eyeliner. There was a strip of masking tape on each locker bearing the name of the occupant. I saw that the stage names at Deja Vu tended toward the unrealistic: "Adore." "Latte." "Nikita." "Dynasty." There wasn't an "Ashley" in sight, I noted with some relief. I preferred the vivid fantasy names to the rich-girl-next-door monikers that were popular at Schieks.

The stickers that decorated nearly every locker were even more revealing than the name tags. They ranged from proud declarations (STRIPPER; SEXY MOM; I HAD YOUR BOYFRIEND) to wry sociopathic statements (YOU SAY TOMATO, I SAY FUCK YOU; MY BITCH GIVES GOOD HEAD; SPEAR BRITNEY!) to ethnic and racial signifiers (PICOSA; COCOA GODDESS; AZIAN PRIDE). I wondered what kind of sticker I'd adhere to my locker, and then I spotted the perfect one: DROPOUT.

"Let me show you the gym and the tanning bed," Sherry said, leading me past the phalanx of lockers.

(The what and the *what*?)

Sherry wasn't being facetious. There were two unoccupied tanning beds, in fact, just off a small mirrored room where ambitious girls attempted tricks on a pair of practice poles. Next door was a small studio with free weights and workout equipment from wall to wall. I was floored by this rare display of dressing-room luxury. While the facilities weren't health-club clean (the whole place seemed to gleam with a varnish of crotch sweat and Bain de Soleil), they were impressive. I wondered if such perks were a common advantage of working for a successful franchise rather than an independent club.

"Here's the Jacuzzi," Sherry announced, gesturing at a large stagnant whirlpool next to the shower area. As if on command, the jets started up and the lapis-colored water began to percolate and froth.

"You guys have a *hot tub*?" I exclaimed. I have always equated hot tubs with hedonism, success and exhaustive fucking. "This place is dope!"

"It don't suck," Sherry concurred.

We headed out of the dressing room into a darkened hallway. "This is the Erotic Loft," she explained, pointing to a pair of locked French doors. "There aren't any surveillance cameras, so a lot of guys like to get their dances in there. It's pricey, like $90 and up."

"What's in there?" I asked.

"Beds," she shrugged. "If you're lucky, you'll spend a lot of time in there. That's where the high rollers go."

I peered through the glass doors, but all I saw were some makeshift curtains rigged to protect the most wayward girls from prying eyes.

Sherry led me into an alcove, revealing a pole that led from the third floor down to the second stage, and an accompanying spiral staircase for the cowardly. "You can take the stairs. I'm gonna pole it," she said. Nonchalantly, she leapt forward, caught the pole in midair and slid down, her thighs squealing against the tarnished brass.

I crept down the staircase and met her at the bottom.

We were standing on the transparent second stage with a panoramic view of the club. Fifteen feet below us, a nude dancer scuttled across the main stage like a blonde sand crab.

"This is the VIP stage," Sherry said. "It doesn't open until the night shift."

"What are those little rooms with the curtains?" I asked, pointing to the back wall adjacent to the bar.

"Those are bedrooms. Where we do the bed dances."

"What's a bed dance?" I asked with trepidation.

"It's like a lap dance, but you lie down on top of the guy and pretend to fuck him. It costs $60. The club counts that as three dances, though, so you have to give them $21," Sherry explained.

"So basically, I get $39 for acting like I'm fucking a dude," I said.

"Yeah, but you're just pretending."

"Groovy."

"There are private lap couches up here, too," Sherry said. The wall was lined with partitioned-off booths; each divider was emblazoned with the image of a woman's fish-net stocking–clad legs. Inside each booth was a small table and a battered love seat. The obvious emphasis on privacy and intimacy at the club was intimidating. Somehow, I wasn't comforted by the tiny security cameras trained on every niche in the room (to say nothing of the areas that deliberately lacked cameras).

Still, I was enchanted by the visceral rock 'n' roll vibe of the joint. The Vu made Schieks and its fake library look positively square. I was also very curious. Was it freaky to slide down those insanely tall poles? Did anyone ever fall down? What actually happened in the Erotic Loft? Did guys actually spend money without alcohol to lubricate their judgment? Deja Vu stank of intrigue and industrial antiseptic.

* * *

Later, I attempted to justify the move as Jonny and I downed Cosmopolitans at the Texa-Tonka. (They only had two martini glasses there, so we were lucky to score the pair for a few hours.)

"Strippers are nomadic by nature," I explained. "No one stays at one club for long. That's why I don't feel bad about leaving Schieks."

"You're going to like Deja Vu a lot better, I think," Jonny said. "The girls there looked cooler. One of them was wearing a nurse costume!"

"I know, right?" I said. "How campy is that?"

"When are you going to tell Schieks you're quitting?" Jonny asked.

"I'm not," I said. "They won't even notice I'm gone."

And from what I hear, they didn't.

Girls, Girls, Girls

"Frankly, I don't think you're going to do well here," the night manager told me from across the bar. His cocaine-duster mustache twitched irritably. "You look mean. You have a very mean look."

"I'm not mean," I spat. My hair was newly dyed bubble-gum pink (which had caused a pleasant ruckus at the office), and I wore a turquoise Lycra playsuit. I had intended to look like an insouciant teen hooker, but apparently my expression was pure punk hostility. I made a mental note to invest in Botox and happy pills.

"You, however, are going to do *very* well," he said to the girl sitting next to me. She was eighteen, lovely and looked like a counselor at a Christian tennis camp. "You've got a docile look. Very sweet, very fresh. The guys love that."

"I've never danced before," she admitted, staring at her lap.

"That's why I'm talking to you two before you start," the manager explained. "I like to explain the procedure to all our new entertainers."

"I've danced before," I volunteered. "At Schieks."

The manager ignored me. "What stage name are you using?" he asked the other girl.

"Nicollette," she said. "It's my sister's name. She's my best friend, and . . ."

"That's a stupid name," Mustache interrupted. "It's not going to work. Pick something sexy, like Diamond."

She nodded, cowed.

"You've got to touch the guys," Mustache barked, running his hand down Diamond's bare back to demonstrate. She stared at the floor. "Walk up to them and say, 'Hey, baby, want to come play with me?' Touch their hair, sit on their laps. You have to be sexy, otherwise you won't make any money." His hand slid down to her thigh. I hastily sipped my soda to curb the gag reflex.

"I can't do that," Diamond said, blanching.

"You'll learn," Mustache insisted. He turned to me. "What's your stage name?"

"*Cherish*," I said. "Because I'm going to cherish every moment we spend together."

He shook his head. "Yeah, okay."

* * *

Diamond and I went up to the second floor stage to practice pole tricks. She looked Junior Miss—perfect with her seamless curtain of Marcia Brady hair and lawn-green bikini. I wondered if Mustache's predictions for our respective successes held water. I didn't think I looked mean. Withdrawn? Perhaps. Inwardly hostile? *Deffo*. But I had assumed my face was a convincing mask of beatific sensuality.

Miss American Pie gripped one of the poles and tried to climb it in her white patent party shoes. She promptly slid down and lost her footing. With her downy limbs crumpled beneath her, she reminded me of Bambi.

"Ow," she said.

"Let me try," I said, executing an awkward spin. I was surprised by how difficult it was. The girls onstage always looked so light and languid when they worked with the pole; by contrast, my body felt like an anthropomorphic sack of wet cat litter. I could barely lift my own weight to leave the floor.

"There must be a trick to this," I said.

A girl emerged from the upstairs dressing room and watched us, her lips curling in amusement. I thought she might introduce herself, but she simply cruised past in a cloud of Thierry Mugler Angel.* Deja Vu was even more impersonal than Schieks due to the volume of dancers who came and went weekly, often without comment either way. The management pressured girls to work as many shifts as they could physically handle, and as a result, there could be fifty girls working on any given night, sometimes more. Also, resting in the dressing room was emphatically

---

* Official scent of Midwestern strippers at the turn of the millennium

discouraged (Vu girls were expected to maintain a continuous hustle), so it was difficult to socialize.

Discouraged by the pole, Diamond and I went back downstairs to check in at the DJ booth. "I really don't think I can do this," she confessed after requesting a Basement Jaxx song. "I can't go up to strange guys and touch them."

"You'll get used to it," I reassured her with all the false wisdom of a five-week stripping veteran. "It's not that bad."

"I guess," Diamond said, nervously fiddling with her clear plastic tip box. Since nude dancers don't customarily wear garters, we'd both brought miniature boxes to carry our tips (as was the custom). Mine was a tin antique that bore the old "Candy Land" board game logo and a photo of two corpulent tots gazing up at a gingerbread house. It seemed like the perfect accessory for such an alluring, artifically sweetened environment. The strippers themselves looked like confections, with their frosted smiles and lollipop-hued costumes. But these were also girls who'd snap your knees like almond bark if you dared to cross them. I knew even little Diamond would eventually harden if she deigned to stick around.

Thus began my tenure at Big Pink. The first thing I noticed was how differently the girls danced compared to Schieks. They didn't just get completely nude; they did full-on gyno shows. I watched as girl after girl sat on the tip rail and pulled her legs open to expose her pussy in scientific detail. Some girls knelt and pulled mens' heads into their expensive man-made cleavage; some picked up dollar bills with their dexterous buttocks, some thrust their crotches against customers' faces and feigned orgasm. One girl dove headfirst into laps and flung her muscular gams over customers' shoulders. The girls who behaved the most outrageously were rewarded with dollar bills, which the customers folded into miniature pyramids of Giza and placed on the tip rail. It reminded me of an auction. *Vagina going once, going twice . . . SOLD to the fellow in the Timberwolves cap and the Manwich-stained fleece pullover!*

I spotted a blonde girl working the floor in an outfit so tight I could clearly see her nipples, labia, individual goose bumps, hair follicles and DNA helix. Her face seemed to have calcified in an expression of pure concentration. Occasionally, she took a customer by the hand and led him upstairs to the beds. The transactions were efficient and joyless, as if she were a bank teller rather than a sex worker. But she had amassed a huge pile of cash, which was bound with a tan rubber band and never left the palm of her hand.

"That's one of the Russians," a passing stripper whispered fearfully, noticing my intense interest in the blonde. (I have what's been described as a "staring problem.") "The Russians always bank. They're unstoppable."

My informant was correct; there was a tight-knit cabal of older Russian women working at Deja Vu, and they were all indestructible flesh-bots. They never accepted "no" from a customer, and they weren't afraid to be pushy or stern. I'd minored in Russian in college*, and I could

---

* Highly useful!

speak the language with some fluency. But I couldn't work up the nerve to address the Russian girls in their native tongue. They were so baldly aggressive that one of them routinely shoved me from behind when she felt I wasn't moving quickly enough across the floor. I wanted to turn around and snarl, "Go back to Kislovodsk, you mail-order cunt!" but I didn't want my cheekbones shattered by Slavic fists of fury. So I kept quiet and pretended to not understand the Russians when they spoke amongst themselves, mumbling stuff like, "Let's pretend to be sick and leave," or, "I dislike the new girl with the brown hair. Did you see her large thighs? It is certain that she feels ashamed of their heft."

The other girls working at the Vu were mostly teenagers. In fact, a couple of them were still in high school (though they had obviously reached the legal stripping age of eighteen). One of them was a cheerleader, and she proudly carried her costumes in a purple-and-gold duffel bag bearing her suburban school's name. She prattled on casually about homework, boys and her hopes that her friends would visit her at the club. To her, stripping was a perfectly acceptable part-time job, and with the exception of her parents, she didn't care who knew about it.

"I just broke off a really long relationship," she told me earnestly as we scanned the floor for gullible types. "We were together almost six weeks."

I couldn't help chuckling. "That doesn't sound too long to me!"

"How old are you?" she asked suspiciously.

"I just turned twenty-five," I said.

"Are you married?" she asked.

"No," I said. "Not yet."

She looked at me like I was an eccentric spinster with birds' nests in my hair. "Wow. I want to get married, like, next year."

"Don't rush it," I said. "Don't rush anything. Enjoy being young and, um, being a stripper, and not having any crushing responsibilities."

"I don't want to be all old and stuff when I have kids," she fretted. "I want to have three by the time I'm your age. Two girls and a boy. I'm going to name them Brianna, Madison and Tyler, and I want to be a stay-at-home mom and . . ."

I shook my head. She reminded me so much of myself and my chick friends when we were seniors in high school, plotting our adult lives down to the most minute detail. The only difference was that this girl routinely got nude and dry-humped guys her father's age. I couldn't blame her for longing to settle down already; she'd probably lived more than the average thirty-year-old. College had to seem like a crashing bore compared to Saturday nights in the Erotic Loft.

"When I was your age, I wanted to be a poet," I said stuffily.

"But you wound up doing this," the girl said. "Why are you here?"

Her question stumped me. I still didn't know what I was doing there. I'd gotten promoted at work, I'd saved enough for a down payment on a Japanese car, and my bizarre little experiment should have been coming to a close. And yet, it continued of my own volition. *Quelle* mindfuck.

* * *

I rose from my bar stool and sauntered over to a man sitting by himself at one of the comically undersized lamplit tables. "How about a bed dance?" I asked, sliding comfortably into his lap as if I were greased in Crisco and utterly fearless.

"Sure," he said, stubbing out his cigarette.

I led him upstairs and into the jungle-themed bedroom. There was a large stuffed leopard on the bed, which I picked up and put on the floor, for lack of a better idea. The man lay down. I took off my top and straddled him, shoving my breasts into his face. His tongue briefly darted into my cleavage and I jumped, but continued the dance. I stared at the mirrored ceiling and watched myself moving rhythmically atop his broad, prone body. I knew I was doing something I never would have considered weeks ago, but I was in a different tribe now.

The man reached into his jeans and adjusted himself so I'd be ideally positioned above his junk. He was frankly turgid. *Watch it, Boner Stabbone*, I thought to myself, but maintained my pained smile. I tried to avoid his erection, but it was impossible to do so without completely rolling off of him. So I pressed my thigh against the hard-on and humped it with my leg until he came. The rush of warmth, and ensuing dark stain, were unmistakable. He sighed with approval, clearly unashamed of the forensic evidence on his 501's.

The ordeal ended quickly, since Deja Vu also customarily faded out songs at the three-minute mark, regardless of whether they were over or not. This was a major rip-off from a customer standpoint, but I was pleased that it meant I'd never be stuck grinding against a guy for all seventeen minutes of "Kashmir." The man paid me my $60 and mumbled a thank-you. Just as he was about to exit the bedroom, a cute waitress appeared in the regulation Deja Vu tank top and sneakers. "Would you like to buy the lady a drink?" she asked.

"All right," the man said, chafed.

"That'll be $9," the waitress said cheerfully. I raised my eyebrows. Nine clams for a lousy glass of cola? The man paid without complaint, and walked away. The waitress handed me a blue ticket along with my soda, which was served in the special tulip-shaped stemware that only the strippers used.

"What is this?" I asked, waving the ticket.

"That's a drink ticket. You turn them in when you leave. Every time a guy buys you a drink, you get a ticket. If you don't have enough tickets by the end of the night, the club will charge you," the waitress said.

I groaned. "You mean I have to convince multiple guys to buy me a $9 pop?"

"Unfortunately, you do," the waitress said. "Some girls deal with it by refusing to give a guy a dance unless he agrees to buy her a drink."

"I can't afford to bargain," I said. "Thanks for clueing me in." I slipped her a couple of bucks and made a mental note: *Enjoy Coke or suffer the consequences!*

"No problem," she said, pivoting in her white sneakers.

* * *

The customers at the Vu were a different breed than the starched golf-outing types who'd frequented Schieks. Some of them seemed downright impoverished. I approached a crumpled fellow who wore a button that said ASK ME ABOUT MY RECENT WEIGHT LOSS.

"So what's all this about your recent weight loss?" I asked. He told me that since he'd joined a notorious vitamin sales cult, he'd gone from taking seven medications for depression to "only five."

"*Only* five," I said. "Wowsers."

"I've made serious progress," he said, knitting his fingers. "I'm down to just lithium and some other things."

"Want a lap dance?" I asked.

"Sorry," he said without a tinge of remorse. "I didn't bring any money. But I have plenty of herbal supplements if you're interested in a trial."

Another guy informed me that he was currently unemployed, but had enjoyed a wildly successful summer mowing lawns.

"I was making great money," he recalled wistfully. "Really mad cash. Too bad the season's over now."

(*But those were heady times, right, man? The hookers and blow, the Kobe beef, the magnums of Cristal at Emilio's summer house? It seemed like the lawns would go on forever, but they never do, man. They never do.*)

By the time a guy described his occupation as "a skate-boarder, sometimes," I was getting exasperated. Where were the businessmen? I longed to see a cash-flush zombie in a Zegna suit, or a rich geriatric or Bob Dobbs from the Church of the Subgenius chewing his pipe with a wink. Many of the customers at Deja Vu wore sweatpants (which was not only aesthetically unpleasant, but created an unpleasantly intimate friction during lap dances). I wasn't elitist; I'd gladly perform for anyone who was willing to pay; but this was like trying to siphon blood from the proverbial turnip. I was beginning to understand why most girls preferred upscale clubs, though I still didn't miss the chatty tedium of Schieks.

* * *

At four-thirty in the morning, the lights finally dimmed. The girls who remained on the floor (many had disappeared to the Erotic Loft hours ago) crowded into the broken elevator and rode upstairs. I crept in among them, so tired that the crowd of girls shimmered like the Painted Desert before my eyes. I could smell their perfume and pheromones and hear them talking in soft, rusty voices about the night's haul. When the elevator doors opened, they flooded into the dressing room, bowlegged from lap dancing, heads down, finally unraveling. *Git along, lil' doggies.* Mellow jazz piano wafted up from downstairs; the DJ liked to play relaxing music at sunrise.

I put on a pair of rubber thongs (which felt oddly collegiate; I hadn't worn footwear to bathe since my freshman dorm) and headed for the showers. As I stood aching beneath the hot spray, another girl lathered up under the adjacent shower head.

"Hi," she said, soaping her fake breasts cheerfully. I almost expected to hear balloon-friction sound effects, like in *Kentucky Fried Movie.* "Did you have a good night?" she asked.

"It was all right," I said, rubbing the crescents of mascara beneath my eyes. "I got twelve dances." To me, this was a decent evening.

"I got twenty-eight," she said casually. "I usually do better."

"May I ask how you do that?" I asked. "I mean, how do you get twenty-eight dances? I've never gotten close to that many."

"I look in the guys' eyes," she said simply. "I look at them real sexy, and then they always want to get a dance from me." She shrugged as if the equation were kindergarten-simple.

"I don't exactly glare at them," I said, toweling off my meager, pendulous breasts. (They were failing me, these tits. They were so damned *anatomical*.)

"Hmm," the girl said. "Well, I guess I don't know how I do it." She tossed her wet taffy-colored hair and grinned at me, guarding her secret like an amulet.

Around 4:30 A.M., the girls reconvened on the main floor for the end-of-shift payout. They curled up like litters of puppies on the couches (greyhound puppies, all limbs), piles of worn-out girls in pajamas, yoga pants, tracksuits and hospital scrubs. Their closeness seemed less like a display of affection than unconscious learned behavior; they'd been snuggling with strange men all night and their physical boundaries were completely worn away. Even I found myself slumped against another girl, who clung to a teddy bear and wore a retainer on her teeth.

Surprisingly, the night wasn't over for most of the strippers. They made breakfast plans, and discussed what they'd do when they got home. "I'm going to have a Valium and take a bath." "I'm going to watch a movie." "I need to get my kids up for school, and then I might sleep a little." Their endurance shocked me, until I realized that I was the most insane person in the room: I had to be at work in three hours.

Which brought me to my next concern: Where the hell were the Mustaches? At Schieks, the payout took all of thirty seconds. You plunked down your share, tipped the floor guys and booked. Here, payout was apparently a complicated event. The managers had to tabulate how much each girl owed the house, a simple exercise in multiplication that mysteriously took forty-five minutes each night to complete. Strangely, no one commented on the excruciating length of this procedure.

"What's going on?" I asked the girl next to me. "Why is this taking so long?"

"The managers like to get fucked up at the end of the night," the girl replied, tapping her nostril. "That's probably what they're doing right now. They don't care if we have to wait around."

"I really need to bail," I said. "I have another job that starts in a couple of hours, and I'm hoping to take a nap."

"Bummer," the girl agreed. "I'm Frost, by the way."

"Hi, Frost. I'm Cherish," I said. I'd noticed Frost on-stage earlier; she moved with a stiff, painful gait. Her stage sets looked like physical therapy.

"How old are you?" she asked me.

"I just turned twenty-five," I told her, "but right now I feel older."

"A lot of people in this business feel older than they are," Frost said. "Look at me. I'm only twenty-two, but I have three kids." She patted her soft, puckered stomach and chuckled ruefully. "I had my legs broken and my teeth knocked out last year when I was pregnant. I had to learn to walk again. I'm still getting the hang of it, as you might have noticed."

"You look great up there," I said.

"Thanks," she said. "Want to see pictures of my kids?" I did. Frost thumbed through a stack of Polaroids, proudly pointing out her cherubic daughters. When we came to a photo of a beetle-browed thug, she kissed it raptly.

"That's my new boyfriend," she said. "He's a Slovakian Jew and has a ten-inch cock."

"Mazel tov!" I said.

"Can you give me a ride to the Starlite Motel?" Frost asked abruptly. "I have to meet someone there in an hour."

"Sorry," I said. "I'm taking a cab home."

Frost rose gingerly and began circling the room, pleading with the other girls for rides. I stretched out on the love seat and closed my eyes. But instead of darkness, I saw an afterimage of girls ascending the spiral staircases flanking the stage, a never-ending parade of marching insects in neon dresses, a lurid Escher. My eyes snapped open.

By the time the managers emerged, lectured us for our lack of enthusiasm and collected our drink tickets and payout, it was 5:00. I climbed into one of the hundreds of cabs I'd take that year, and rode home in silence. I was starting to not feel tired anymore. I wondered if I'd be able to sustain the wired feeling and slog through a long day at the agency. When I got home and undressed, I realized that my legs were covered in violent-looking bruises, blue and yellow and flowering wildly down my calves like a Georgia O'Keeffe rendered in internal bleeding. Such were the risks of pole and floor work.

* * *

I worked my can off at Deja Vu two nights a week, and spent the following mornings in a somnambulatory trance. The shifts lasted nine hours, sometimes ten, and I spent the bulk of that time tirelessly hustling. I also danced about six sets per night, either on the main stage or upstairs in the "exclusive" VIP room (which, puzzlingly, was free and open to the public). Bed dances were a regular part of my nightly routine, and I learned to vary my crotch pressure subtly in order to maintain a customer's state of arousal without prematurely blowing the transaction. I knew that what I was doing was akin to a $60 hand job, but I felt like one of the cool girls when I scored repeat dances from some throbbing schmuck. There were occupational hazards, though, like the Mexican guy who bit my tit and drew blood, or the tourist from Bombay who tried with near-success to stick his fingers inside me, or the guy from Detroit who whipped out his dick and tried to shove my face onto it, laughing as I thrashed in horror. (On all three occasions, my manager scolded me for "allowing" these assaults to happen.)

And then there was the indignity of "up time": After every four songs, all the dancers were required to line up on the main stage, at which point the DJ would introduce us as we waved mutely like auto-show bikini models. After the introduction, we were supposed to exit the stage, disperse and solicit two-for-one lap dances as quickly as we could. The girls who didn't have any takers were required to return to the stage and dance en masse for the next two songs, a mortifying ritual known among the strippers as "the loser dance" or "loser stage." If you missed an introduction, or failed to participate in the loser dance, you could be fined. (The managers were far more likely to fine girls they didn't like, trust or habitually fuck, and I fit the bill in all respects.)

I occasionally rushed up to my locker for a clandestine protein fix (beef jerky, consumed quickly so no one would see my food and beat me up for it prison-style), but the managers had a foul habit of bursting into the dressing room and shouting at us to get our asses back downstairs. Sometimes I was even afraid to pee, since the Mustaches didn't seem too humane for a midstream sabotage. I imagined them breaking down the stall with a phallic battering ram, their nostrils frothing with cocaine.

One night I got sick. You might say I was in intestinal distress. (Okay, I had explosive, pyrotechnic diarrhea. Pretty!) This presented a couple of problems: First of all, there were only two toilets in the dressing room; they were adjacent to the hot tub and far from private. The last thing I needed was to be scorned by strippers for daring to "drop a deuce" (thus destroying the collective illusion that we were all sterile, fragrant fuck-dolls incapable of eating or excreting). The second problem was the extreme difficulty inherent in stripping when one is wracked with abdominal cramps.

I wanted to go home, but I'd heard that girls could be fined up to $180 for skipping out on a shift. Quitting was an ever-present option, and yet I knew, somehow, that the ride wasn't over and I couldn't pull the brake just yet. I locked myself in the toilet and hoped the Mustaches wouldn't find me or fine me. That was one of the first times it occurred to me that I was working in a pink gulag. I suspected that the Mustaches would rather see my lower intestine fall out of my ass onstage than allow me to go home. Outside, someone banged on the stall. "Loser dance, honey. Get downstairs."

Sugar Low

Regardless of the fact that I spent my nights grabbing my ankles for absentee husbands, I still aspired to be premium girlfriend material. Loving Jonny was easy: He played guitar, he cooked a revelatory Tater Tot hotdish, he wore Ben Sherman shirts, he wasn't a carrier of commitment-phobia or other notable boy diseases and he used expensive moisturizer. That's about all it takes to bang my gong. Plus, his daughter, whom he addressed as Peanut, was starting to grow on me in a weird way. This was a slow and circuitous process, like a seed germinating in a Dixie cup.

Peanut was the original candy girl, a bona fide sugar fiend. Actually, she'd eat anything sweet. Pancake syrup. ChapStick. The vitamin-fortified silt in the bottom of the Cocoa Puffs box. She spent most evenings staring at my personal stash of lollies and pleading for a fix. I usually relented, because candy made her grin like a movie star.

One night, the girl was eight miles high on Pez and Pop Rocks and Jonny couldn't get her to sleep. No amount of Beatles medleys could lure the little monkey into the arms of Morpheus; she was a hot mess and growing increasingly manic. While Peanut zoomed on sucrose and Jonny struggled to subdue her, I watched *Letterman* and felt strangely enervated. Compared to the buzz of stripping, everyday life flatlined on my radar and bored me to sobs. Drag city, man.

"I don't wanna sleep," Peanut announced shrilly in her bedroom. "I want pizza. And I want . . . the MALL OF AMERICA!" Jesus, what a snapshot.

"It's bedtime," Jonny said soothingly. "All little girls need their sleep."

"Not me!" Peanut shrieked, kicking her mattress in waltz time.

Jonny began crooning "Eleanor Rigby," arguably the most morbid song in the Beatles catalog but a longtime Peanut favorite. Slowly, the protests subsided and the butterfly kicks slowed like a heartbeat. After nearly an hour, Jonny's kid finally began to snore.

Jonny shut Peanut's bedroom door quietly. "Sorry about that parental moment, babe."

"Understood," I said. I knew that when Peanut was over, I was relegated to the deli bin just opposite chopped liver. That's part and parcel of the stepmom gig, if you want to hear it straight.

"I'm also sorry that her mom left that angry note on your windshield this morning," Jonny said.

"Vastly preferable to the usual angry voice mails," I

replied. Peanut's mom didn't dig me too much. She had this irrational suspicion that I was too motherly toward her child, which was super hilarious. I had the maternal instinct of a grouper. I even felt weird holding Peanut's hand when we crossed the street, like things were moving too fast and I needed to see other toddlers.

"Yeah, that's not cool, either," Jonny conceded, joining me on the divan and filching a pizza roll from my plate.

"It bugs," I said. "But then, so does everything lately."

Despite our best intentions, our rented domicile had become a Roman circus of late. Jonny, though darling, was a man with enough heavy baggage to pitch a 767 into the Baltic Sea. Evidently, he wasn't divorced on paper (surprise!), and the acrimonious proceedings were still underway. Jonny is a fellow who avoids conflict at any cost, so it didn't surprise me that he'd never finalized the split. What did surprise me was how guilty I felt about rogering someone else's husband every night.

By moving to Minneapolis, I'd unwittingly walked into an emotional abattoir that would have reduced even the coolest cuke to pulp. Maybe I deserved to get screwed. It's gloriously stupid to move in with a dude—a *dad*—who's married to someone else, even in the antiseptic legal sense. Jonny was adamant that he loved my ass, but he was also haunted by the possibility of losing his little Peanut because of me.

I felt sorry for Jonny. He'd been brought up Lutheran and the concept of penance (or spiritual bribery) was alien to him. Me, I'd been reared to believe that ten Hail

Marys, a couple of Our Fathers and a Fleet enema could mend the hairline fractures in a guilty conscience. However, thirty thousand petitions to the inviolate Virgin couldn't absolve me of my alleged crime: the willful dissolution of a family. I'd shat on the sixth commandment, and I'd have to grind out the sin with my hips. I'd complete the first all–lap dance rosary in recorded history, bead by bead, joint by joint. Besides, if I was going to be branded an adulteress, I was going to act like it.

Fake Plastic Hair

After a few weeks of Deja Vu, I decided to buy a blonde wig. I had just gotten phony French fingernail extensions (applied by a Korean youth using illegal methyl methacrylate) and I decided to take the stripper look all the way to the stratosphere. A blonde wig would complete my transformation, and (I hoped) make me rich. I refused to accept that my lack of success was owing to my attitude or dearth of confidence. I firmly believed the issue was purely physical, and could be remedied once I assumed a more Barbie-like form.

I went to a depressing pink-and-gray wig salon in a third-tier shopping mall. It was the kind of mall where the fountains ceased operation years ago and the anchor stores are rapidly liquidating their inventory. The wig salon was more evocative of chemotherapy treatments than glamour makeovers, but I was too impatient to shop around. I was planning to strip that evening, and I wanted to do it with my fantasy hair. I would snare customers in my golden locks and bind them until they were purple and gasping. Then, I'd grab their wallets and run cackling into the night. Rapunzel the rapist. Fucking *right on.*

The two bored teenage girls minding the store noshed on veggie subs and gossiped in low tones. They smiled when I entered, but didn't offer any assistance. I strolled the perimeter of the store, grimacing at the Carol Brady mullets, hot-roller shags and plasticene bobs on the hauntingly featureless Styrofoam heads.

"Do you have anything that isn't totally ugly?" I asked the girls.

"Most of the people who come here are old ladies with no hair," one of them answered derisively. "So we don't really have anything good."

"There's some longer stuff over there," the other one offered, pointing to a corner of the store. I spotted a long, ash-blonde wig with bangs. The color reminded me of Krystle from *Dynasty,* but the style was more *Alice in Wonderland.* I took the wig off its assigned head and tried it on. Startling. The length of the wig elongated my face and emphasized my nose, which wasn't exactly the effect I'd had in mind. However it was pale and silky and innocent, which was precisely the image I wanted to project. Also, it was made of human hair (creepy!) and felt realistic, despite the fact that it looked totally hinky.

"I'm going to take this one," I said.

"That'll be $99," one of the girls said, folding the wig into a bag. I gulped and paid in dirty cash, inwardly reassuring myself that the investment would pay for itself many times over.

That night in the Deja Vu dressing room, I did my makeup differently. I lined my eyes heavily in black kohl (Estée Lauder, the best to be had), patted my eyelids with bruise-colored shadow (Benefit Traffic School) and applied pale beige lipgloss (Urban Decay Midnight Cowboy), the color of which reminded me of a prosthetic leg. The effect was very *Playboy,* flaxen and atonal, with eyes so sooty that I looked like I'd been slugged by a jealous rock star at Chateau Marmont. I put on a mesh wig cap and pulled the wig over it. I was like an entirely different person, much to my delight.

I took the back stairway (which, in an amusing attempt at ambience, contained a single potted palm with a price tag still dangling from it) and pranced down to the main floor. Immediately, one of the blonde Russian girls (Sasha? Oksana? Sashkana?) charged up to me.

"Are you new girl?" she demanded.

"No, I'm Cherish," I said, grinning like a skull. *Success!*

Sashkana raised her eyebrows, which were intimidating Gothic arches fashioned of MAC brow pencil. "Cherish? I didn't recognize you!"

"I bought a wig," I said dumbly. "I'm incognito."

"Is good wig," Sashkana concluded. "Yeah, is good wig."

"Thanks bunches for the vote of confidence," I said. "Blondes have more fun, right?"

Sashkana pondered the cliché, and frowned as if she

hadn't had fun in years. "Maybe. I dunno. Some girls. Not me."

* * *

Predictably, I sold my first lap dance of the night to a man who was enchanted with my phony blonde head.

"You have such beautiful hair," he said as I straddled him and humped his semierect junk with vigor. "Are you Swedish?"

"Yes," I said. "I'm one hundred percent Swedish. In fact, I was just whale-watching in Stockholm with my friends Bjorn and Annika. Then we picked lingonberries and lashed each other with thorns and twigs. Thank goodness for subsidized health care."

The man closed his eyes contentedly. "You're so hot."

"Like a meatball, right?" I said, bouncing gaily on his lap. *Blonde, blonde, blonde! Whee!* "Am I your little Swedish meatball?"

"Absolutely," the guy said. "In fact, I'd like another dance, if you're not busy right now."

"I'm in high demand," I said, "but I have such a crush on you that I couldn't possibly walk away." He smiled and arched his crotch hard against my pelvic bone, as though he wanted me to mash his cock to a pulp.

I kept fairly busy as the night rolled on, though I wasn't as staggeringly successful as I'd hoped. At one point, I approached a wholesome-looking, sweatshirt-clad young man, hunkered down next to his table, and asked him if he'd like a lap dance.

"No, thank you. My friends brought me here, but this

just isn't my scene," he explained as I knelt on the floor like a spaniel begging for Snausages. "I'm getting married in six days, and I'm more interested in my fiancée than I am in strippers."

"Wow," I said with sincerity. "That's really refreshing."

"My fiancée may not be as beautiful as you girls," he said. "But she's a good, honest person."

That gave me pause. Even though the man obviously thought he was speaking highly of his fiancée, I couldn't help but think that she'd be insulted. Just as strippers balk at being stereotyped as amoral, damaged sluts, no "civilian" woman wants to be thought of solely as obedient, sexless and wholesome. I could tell by the man's disapproving expression that he couldn't imagine his faithful wife-to-be as belonging to the same tribe as the lip-licking birds of paradise who splayed themselves across the Deja Vu stage. But she could have been one of us, even if he didn't realize it. There were some good, honest people running around at the strip club; most were just well hidden under an impenetrable mantle of makeup and Mystic Tan.

"Well, good luck in your marriage," I said. "Maybe you should bring your wife here some time."

"Oh, she'd never come here," the man said, assured of the purity of his betrothed.

*   *   *

I noticed something strange as the night wore on: The other girls at the club were a lot friendlier to me since I'd been reincarnated as a blonde. It was like I'd joined the

Aryan sisterhood. Suddenly, I was privy to backstage gossip and instructions on how to execute the latest pole maneuvers. I had assumed that my wig would elicit a chilly reaction from the girls (since it would ostensibly make me a more formidable competitor on the floor), but the opposite was true. Now I was a contender, and therefore worthy of respect and friendship. The strippers drew their enemies close to their immobile, silicon-cutlet bosoms, and ignored most everyone else.

* * *

Around 1:00 A.M., one of the Mustaches cornered me.

"Can you do a panty auction in VIP?" he asked me. "No one else is available."

"Sure," I said, pleased to be the last-resort panty-auctioneer-of-choice. "How does that work?"

"We give you a pair of Deja Vu panties to wear. You go onstage for two songs, and the guys at the tip rail bid on your panties. The guy who puts down the most money gets them."

"I can do that," I said. Mustache tossed a pair of green satin panties at me. They had shamrocks on them (it was June) and fit like a diaper, but I figured I could make do.

"Guys, now's the time to head up to the VIP room for a chance to win Cherish's panties!" the DJ hollered into the mic. He always sounded so smug because lots of strippers were fucking him.

I took the stage, and was greeted with surprisingly hearty applause. The tip rail in VIP wasn't very large, but it was crowded with drunk university boys who grinned as though it were Christmas morning and Santa had brought them a sleigh loaded with semiconscious *Hustler* honeys. I smiled and smoothed my Irish diaper enticingly. (Remember those old Victoria's Secret satin bikini panties that always looked pouchy in the ass? These panties were exactly like that.)

"Give 'em to me!" a boy shouted, laying a five-dollar bill on the rail. On the other side of the stage, another boy retaliated by constructing an elaborate pyramid of folded singles.

"The pyramid guy is winning," I declared, dancing up to the front lip of the stage and twirling around the pole. "I award extra points for effort." I figured I'd make the bastards *work* for my skanky green drawers, you know?

In response, the first guy pulled out more money and laid it down. He pointed to his chest wildly. "Pick me! I gotta have your panties!"

The pyramid guy's creation increased from modest Mayan scale to ancient Egyptian grandeur as he added more dollars. He smiled at me conspiratorially. A few more guys pulled out money, eager to join the competition. They began tossing handfuls of money at the stage, which I wallowed through delightedly, shuffling the bills about like dead leaves. I was literally ankle deep in cash, and it kept coming. The sound of legal tender hitting my legs was exquisite.

The second song began. I pulled off the panties and dangled them teasingly in front of the tip rail. Naked but for my black stilettos, I sat down on the edge of the stage, leaned back and spread my legs for the big finish. A flying dollar hit me square in the crotch. I scooted backward onto the stage and began rolling around dramatically in the scattered pile of money. (I couldn't pass up an *Indecent Proposal* moment.)

"Panties! Panties!" the guys chanted. I waved the panties in response, giggling as I writhed in my bed of crumpled money. This was the zenith of my adult sexual life. Had I even lived before I'd auctioned off my underthings?

"Time's up for the panty auction!" the DJ's voice boomed from downstairs. "Panties going once . . . going twice . . . sold!"

I yanked back the waistband slingshot-style and let the panties fly at the pyramid guy. The other guys groaned in disappointment. I squatted on my haunches and struggled to collect all my money. The mess of bills was almost too much to carry, but somehow I didn't care. A couple of strippers passing through the VIP room stopped to gawk. I waved and ran naked up the stairs to the dressing room, flush with power.

My first night as a synthetic blonde had been a moderate success, though I still hadn't earned nearly as much as the other ho's in my area code. I knew this because the Mustaches made everyone's earnings public. During payout each night, they'd rapidly read off how much each girl owed the house (and if you happened to miss your name and ask them to repeat, they'd call you "retarded"). Anyway, using rudimentary math, one could easily calculate how much a stripper had earned based on what she owed. When someone owed more than several hundred dollars, you knew she had buh-buh-BANKED. Sometimes I owed as little as $80. This presented a veritable Mobius strip of gnarled logic: While I was pleased that my payouts were usually minimal, I also wished that they were massive, since that would mean I was a stone-cold pimp. Some girls liked the fact that Deja Vu adjusted their take according to individual earnings, but I was starting to view it as a scam. The more you earned, the more they socked away. Whether you had a lousy night or a fantastic night, you were fucked.

*   *   *

In addition to periodic raucous panty auctions, another nightly ritual at Deja Vu was the "chair torture." A bachelor or birthday boy would be summoned onstage and made to sit in an unspeakably filthy chair propped against the center pole. The strippers, who were all required to participate, would stand in a V-formation like psychedelic geese and clap in unison to "We Want Some Pussy" by 2 Live Crew. Meanwhile, the more outgoing girls took turns jumping on the bachelor, whapping him in the face with their tits and kneeing him in the junk. Sometimes a girl would pull off the guy's belt and beat him with it. The routine could get surprisingly violent, and the "victims' " reactions ranged from merely uncomfortable to straight-up pissed. *Happy birthday, motherfucker! You're about to be the target of twenty strippers' pent-up rage against men!* Because Deja Vu was a popular party destination, "chair torture" could occur up to ten times a night. As a result, I unwittingly memorized every word to "We Want Some Pussy." I still hate that song.

Slippery When Wet

I never worked at the Vu on Wednesday nights, but one week I deliberately made an exception. Wednesday was "Wet 'n' Wild Night" (sponsored by O'Douls, the tonic of teetotalers) and I wanted to see what exactly this mysterious watery theme entailed.

"Oh, Wet 'n' Wild," a girl said when I asked her about it. "It's gross."

"Totally nasty," another girl concurred. "They pick three or four girls to run around onstage, and the audience gets to squirt them."

"I sort of like it," a third girl admitted. "It's a nice break from the norm. Actually, I usually volunteer."

My curiosity piqued, I scheduled myself for a Wednesday. The night began as usual, but around 10:00 P.M., a bouncer began handing out plastic squirt bottles and water pistols to the boisterous crowd at the tip rail. The Vu got a lot of college students, which displeased me; they were abominable tippers and seemed to have a distinct preference for whispery-voiced airhead strippers who could make them feel intelligent by comparison. The median age of the crowd that had gathered for Wet 'n' Wild was around nineteen. The kids gripped their squirt bottles with excited aggression, as if they were ready to play a triple-X version of cops and robbers.

"Gentlemen, no squirting in the face," the DJ announced. "Ladies, come on out!"

Three girls ran onstage wearing oversized Deja Vu T-shirts. Two of them were pocket-sized Asian girls, and the tacky tees hung past their knees like avant-garde Yohji Yamamoto dresses. The third girl was a robust blonde with 400-cc funbags, and I saw a few of the guys identify her as their favorite by taking aim immediately.

"Ready, set, go!" the DJ proclaimed. Now, I had naively assumed that this exercise was simply a glorified wet T-shirt contest. However, the shirts served little purpose, because the girls immediately lifted them up to their chins, exposing their naked bodies beneath. Streams of water arced through the air as the girls skipped around the stage. The room was filled with the mechanical *sklish-sklish-sklish* sound of twenty squirt bottles being furiously operated at once.

The two Asian girls sat down in front of the tip rail and pulled their legs behind their heads. The guys instantly began squirting their pussies and rectums. It reminded me of a game of chance at a carnival: *Hit the anus and win a stuffed unicorn for your sweetie!* I noticed the water was going directly into the girls' vaginas in some cases. It was the world's first interactive douche!

Water pooled on the stage; the strippers were soaking wet. The girls pulled off the dripping T-shirts and hurled them into the crowd. One of the little Asian girls got on all fours while the other one mounted her and pretended to fuck her in the ass. Obviously feeling left out, the blonde girl knelt behind the dominant Asian girl and faked eating her pussy from behind. The three of them collapsed into a slippery pile and pawed each other, their fake giggles progressing to fake hysterics as the action intensified. Asses were grabbed. Nipples were tweaked. Tongues were unfurled for some of the showiest kissing I've ever seen.

"Thank you, ladies!" the DJ announced. The girls quickly collected the soggy bills that ringed the stage and ran upstairs to the dressing room. A pockmarked kid was summoned to mop up the excess water. I watched the boys at the rail reluctantly return their squirt bottles to the bouncer. I envied them; they'd paid a few bucks at the door for the privilege of dousing a trio of beautiful naked women with frigid water. There had been no limitations or mystery; the girls had literally invited them to squirt body parts that most women only see when their gynecologist holds up that stupid hand mirror. The boys' faces had been so blank, their trigger fingers spasming relentlessly as they stared between the girls' splayed thighs. I'd seen that face before, on an ex-boyfriend when he played video games. Empty. No one home but the id.

Activity Korner!

Match the stripper's preferred music with her personality type. (Results were compiled after an extended study at several clubs.)

1. The Eagles

2. Mariah Carey

3. Creed

4. Rammstein

5. *Erotica*-era Madonna

a. Good-natured alcoholic

b. Ugly face, nice hair

c. Methadone clinic patron

d. Bitch

e. Friendly Canadian hesher

Answers: 1. b., 2. a., 3. d., 4. e., 5. c.

Some Girls

To my surprise, I got promoted to assistant project manager at the agency. It was the first job I'd ever had that involved actual responsibility and accountability. Although I accepted the promotion graciously, I was secretly horrified. I'd enjoyed being a copy typist. It was the kind of bare-bones, solitary, no-"team"-in-"I"-type job I gravitated toward as a sociopath. I'd type scripts at mercurial speeds, hand them off and resume my intense e-mail badinage with Jonny ("I want you inside me. Yours, Diablo"). But now, I had to do actual work and deal with other people. I knew I was up shit creek *sans* paddle when my boss showed me how to organize a "job file." (I'm the kind of person who accidentally puts the TV remote in the vegetable crisper, so the idea of me keeping documents orderly is *hilarious*.)

The only plus side to getting promoted was the promise of more money in my faux-croc wallet. I had become financially dependent on stripping, and the proverbial "golden handcuffs" were beginning to chafe. I'd always thought the income I earned would simply result in piles of fun money, but we spent it as quickly as I earned it. I bought a car and funneled increasing quantities of money into my fantastic plastic appearance: high-end makeup, hair extensions and enough bikinis to fill a giant shopping bag in my closet. Rather than a way of earning extra cash, stripping had become a necessary source of income, and quitting wasn't in my budget. Jonny and I lived from paycheck to paycheck, and the only thing that afforded us a modicum of comfort was my new hobby. I couldn't quit, even though I hated Deja Vu so much that the mere thought of that bismuth-pink building made my teeth hurt.

* * *

It was around 1:00 A.M. on a molasses-slow Monday night. I had netted around $75 for seven hours of work, a pathetic, wretched sum that would be dubbed "McDonald's money" by all but the most desperate stripper. I trolled the room for potential customers, exhausted. Crueler still, the other girls seemed to be doing a brisk business. There were plenty of guys in the house, but they weren't exactly clamoring for the pleasure of my company. (Shocking, since I'm sure I looked like Helen of Troy with my slumped shoulders, matted wig, and skintight booty shorts that cleaved my crotch into two distinct visible halves; it was X-Treme Camel Toe.)

As I headed backstage dejectedly, a young guy in a *Wild*

America neckbeard stepped in front of me, forcing me to stop. He'd been tossing cash at the stage all night and this was the first time I'd seen him abandon his seat at the tip rail.

"Hi," I said warily, anticipating his query: *The bathroom is down that corridor, first door on the right.*

The guy's face was expressionless. "You are very beautiful," he said in a thick foreign accent. "Will you do a bed dance for me?"

"Sure," I said happily. I'd been clamoring for just $20; I'd be ecstatic to get $60. I didn't particularly like doing bed dances, but I'd become accustomed to the drill of humping guys' lunch boxes with my thigh while they stared passively at my breasts hanging overhead like forbidden kumquats.

I took the man by his clammy hand and led him upstairs. (The Mustaches told us to always hold hands with the customers when escorting them about.) "So, where are you from?" I asked.

"Russia," he said.

"I speak Russian somewhat well," I tentatively volunteered in Russian.

"Your accent is excellent," he replied in Russian, surprised. "Where did you learn that?"

"I studied the language at, um, an Iowan university. A university in Iowa," I fumbled in broken Russian. I hadn't spoken the language in two years.

"I'm impressed," the Russian said, switching back to English.

"Thanks," I said. "Shall we begin the dance?"

* * *

After three songs had ended, the Russian requested a fourth bed dance. I was about to comply when he paused and sat up, contemplating the surveillance camera. They were mounted on the ceiling in each second-floor "bedroom."

"What's up?" I asked, desperate to continue my run.

"I was thinking," the Russian said. "There are no cameras upstairs, right? On your third floor?"

"Yeah," I said carefully. "There aren't any cameras in the Erotic Loft."

"What can we do up there that we can't do here?" he asked.

"More," I said quickly. I didn't want to specify, since I didn't want to *do* more, but I was hungry. Ravenous. I knew going up to the Erotic Loft would guarantee me at least $90 (bed dances up there were $30 apiece with three-dance minimum). I had never been asked to go upstairs before, and I felt like I'd received a bid for an exclusive nude sorority. (Hair Pi?) I didn't feel like playing the tired role of Little Miss Good Judgment this evening and ever after. I wanted to go upstairs. I was going upstairs.

As we walked up the chilly back stairway, I braced myself for my first inside glimpse of the infamous Loft. We entered the pitch-dark, cavernous room through the glass-paned French doors. Upon our entry, an attendant with a flashlight phoned down to the DJ to inform him that I wouldn't be available to go onstage until further notice. I was disappointed to see that the much-touted "theme rooms" were merely small, dark areas partitioned off with black lace curtains, like Spanish mantillas. We entered one of the areas, and I noticed that the wall above the rumpled bed was spattered with a mysterious white substance. It looked like a crime scene or a cheap theater set.

The Russian laid down on the bed. "Can you take off all your clothes?" he asked.

"I'm not supposed to," I said, but I did it anyway.

A waitress suddenly drew aside the lace curtain and peeked in at us. "Would you like to buy the lady a drink?" she asked the Russian dutifully, but her eyes were fixed on me. I stood stark naked and stared back at her like Edvard Munch's *Puberty*. We were mutually ashamed. It was almost as if we holding a psychic debate. Resolved: My job is shittier than yours.

"I'll have a Diet Coke," I replied. She nodded and stole away in her spotless white sneakers.

"Take your shoes off, too," the Russian said. I kicked off my black platforms, the ones Jonny had picked out for me the preceding weekend, and crawled on top of the Russian. I heard faint laughter coming from one of the other sectioned-off rooms. I recognized the deep, bittersweet chuckle as belonging to a hulk of a stripper named Katrine who looked like a drag queen and blew guys for hydroponic pot. I was in Katrine's world now, but I lacked the protection of that rough, jaded laugh that stirred the ashes in her lungs. Katrine wasn't scared of anything; she cared for herself above all else. Compared to her, I was a scared little bitch with dirty panties. *Channel Katrine,* I told myself. She laughed again, and it sounded like an Eartha Kitt record skipping.

It felt like a dream. I did what I did for one reason: I wanted every last kopek of the Russian's seemingly limitless fortune. I wanted to be one of the girls who went home with hundreds, maybe thousands of dollars. I didn't need to be that girl every night, but I felt entitled to wear the crown just once. Not so much for the money itself, but for the status, the reassurance that I measured up. The Russian lowered his jeans. Three songs went by, and the Russian asked me to keep going. I did, mentally calculating how much he owed me. Six songs. Nine songs. Twelve songs. My hips ached, ball grinding against socket, but I kept going. And went further. I found that singing along with the ridiculous piped-in pop music made it easier to continue, and the Russian didn't seem to mind. So I sang my heart out, bracing myself on the wall with outstretched palms and wincing as the Russian groped me: *"I'm like a bird, I'll only fly away . . ."*

* * *

After about forty minutes spent horizontal, I felt the uncontrollable urge to bolt. "I have to go," I lied. "I'm supposed to be onstage in a few minutes."

"But I'm not finished," the Russian said, stroking my belly.

"I know," I said. "I can get you another girl."

The Russian pulled out his red croc wallet and handed me a sizable wad of twenties and fifties. I pulled on my hot pants, grabbed the one shoe I was able to locate in the dark and stumbled barefoot toward the dressing room. A brand-new girl named Lolly, a teenager who had never stripped before prior to that night, was leaving the dressing room in a plaid jumper just as I entered.

"Hey," I said, seizing her by the shoulders. "There's a guy in the Loft that asked me to send in another girl for him. He's got loads of money. Go now."

"How will I find him?" Lolly asked, terrified.

"First bed," I said. "Go." I felt somewhat guilty about throwing young Lolly to Tchaikovsky's drooling wolf, but somehow I knew she'd thank me later. (She did.)

*　*　*

At four-thirty, we all commenced our usual slow-motion ritual of undressing, sloughing off eyeliner and tending to nascent blisters. I was crouching naked in front of my locker and eating a slice of pizza (sexy!) when the meaner Mustache burst into the dressing room, his eyes wild.

"Don't get dressed," he ordered us, fiddling with his cheap-ass Gingiss Formalwear tie. "We have some important guys that just showed up and I need girls onstage."

"It's fucking five in the morning!" a girl named Ally yelped as she straddled a comically oversized douche.

"I don't care," Mustache said, and left.

"This is so stupid," I heard one of the strippers bitch as soon as Mustache was out of earshot. "They always keep the place open for the high rollers. It's not fair. They're gonna go up to the Loft anyway, so who cares if we're on-stage or not?"

"Lainy and Fantasia must have been clued in that they were coming," another girl said. "Did you see how they were waiting by the door all night? Greedy bitches. I hope they suck those guys' dicks quick so we can go home."

"Next onstage, we're going to have Cherish!" the DJ yelled downstairs, obviously as irritated with this development as anyone.

"What?" I said. "I only have one shoe! I lost the other one in the Loft."

"Go look for it," one of the girls suggested.

"No time," I said. "The shoe's probably up someone's ass by now."

"Once again, here's Cherish," the DJ repeated, annoyed.

"Fuck it," I said. Without bothering to get dressed or borrow a pair of shoes, I walked naked and barefoot downstairs and onto the stage. The big main room was as cold and empty as an airplane hangar. I smiled at Mustache, who glared at me from behind his omnipresent clipboard. If they wanted me to dance at daybreak, I was going to really dance. The DJ played "Scar Tissue" by the Red Hot Chili Peppers, and I improvised a ballet.

I did arabesques and pirouettes and *changements*. I leapt like Baryshnikov, not caring how my imperfect body chose to ripple or respond to the crash landings. My vanity was gone, replaced with regret and exhaustion and the strange creeping clarity of dawn. In my bare feet, I could be far more graceful than in those crippling stilettos. I whirled and twirled and caressed the poles as if they were a gauntlet of handsome partners. I laughed aloud when I realized how horrified my parents would be if they knew that nine years of childhood ballet lessons had come to this. Spontaneous naked choreography on a dirty stage at sunrise.

"Thank you, Cherish," the DJ said drily.

* * *

When my trusty Rainbow cab finally dropped me off at home, the sky was a buttery color. I wasn't sure I'd be able to sleep at all before my alarm went off at 7:00 for work.

"Morning, baby doll," Jonny murmured sleepily as I crept into the bedroom like a thief.

"Hi," I whispered. "I missed you so much tonight."

"How did you do?" Jonny asked, rolling over onto his back.

"I made a lot of money. A lot. More than I've ever made," I said, releasing my death grip on the Lunch Box of Ill-Gotten Gains.

"What did you do?" Jonny asked, interested. Shocker: I could hear a grin in his voice. The insane thing about Jonny is that he always understood why shit happened. He treated my shifts at the club like any night of wholesome (albeit kinky) hard labor, and never imparted them with any unnecessary emotional meaning. The proverbial green-eyed monster never made an appearance in our relationship. Jonny's trust in me extended beyond the superficial, mechanical actions of my body; he never doubted my extreme devotion to him or the pyrotechnics he still managed to inspire in my tired loins at five a.m. I didn't know a single stripper who was lucky enough to have such an honorable dude.

"It's so nasty," I said, crawling into bed. "You really want to know?"

"Yes," Jonny said.

I told him the entire story about the Russian. "I mean, is that cool? Does that freak you out?"

"No," Jonny said, wrapping his arms around me. "In fact, I'll probably masturbate to that image for weeks. You are one dirty bird, darling."

"I'll never do that again," I said truthfully. "I know it went way too far."

"Well, you don't have to do it again," Jonny said. "But you did it this time, and you shouldn't feel ashamed about it."

I relaxed in the darkness. "Okay. I promise not to enter a shame spiral."

"Were you afraid you'd get caught?" Jonny asked.

"Sort of," I said. "I mean, we're not supposed to be totally nude anywhere but onstage. Nudity with contact is *verboten*. And I mean . . . well, I could have gotten fired for a lot of things. I . . ."

"My girl breaks all the rules," Jonny mumbled, falling asleep again.

The Ten Worst Stripper Names

1. Edwidge

2. Chlamydia

3. Your sister's name

4. Fatwa

5. Junqui

6. Britney, Brittanee, Britni, Brittanie, etc.

7. Zqwzybrk (pronounced "Britney")

8. Placenta

9. Dysplasia

10. Stayfree

The Girl from Ipanema

At three o'clock in the morning one Thursday, I found myself soaking my feet in the polluted Jacuzzi with a Brazilian girl named Joni. She was wearing a cheap Swiss maid costume that, paired with her Brazilian accent, was endearingly ridiculous. Joni had the kind of thick, unyielding body that looked like it had been carved from a single cord of wood. She wasn't thin, but she was monument-solid in an attractive way.

"I was supposed to be a clown," she announced as the water rose past our ankles. "My father is a clown. Everyone is my family does clowning."

"Stripping is kind of like being a clown," I offered. "I was just onstage in VIP, and these guys weren't tipping, so I started dancing the Robot. Then one of them put a Sacagawea dollar coin on the tip rail and I pretended to put it in my butt."

Joni smiled and shook her head. "No, being a clown is

very noble. You can perform for people who have cancer and things."

"Having cancer is bad enough," I said. "But cancer *and* things? That's when I question the existence of God."

"Would you like a bonbon, Cherish?" Joni asked me suddenly. "I am pregnant and I am craving chocolate all the time. They are Ferrero Rocher." She pronounced *Ferrero Rocher* in such an intoxicating way, like the name of a charismatic dictator; I couldn't possibly decline.

"Thanks," I said, accepting the warm, malformed truffle from the pocket of her apron.

"I don't think I'll have the baby," Joni sighed. "I'm only eighteen and I don't have, you know, an American diploma." I noticed she wore a thick gold ring on her finger that said *JESUS* in block script.

"Tough decision," I said. "I'm twenty-five, and I'm still scared of babies."

"I'm scared of abortion," Joni said. "Do you know who is lucky? My cousin. She is marrying a man who looks exactly like Seann William Scott from the movie *American Pie 2*. He is very cute. They are going to have a baby."

"I'm sure you'll have your own baby someday," I offered.

"I hope so," Joni said. She slipped farther into the Jacuzzi, and the water burbled around the frilly hem of her Heidi costume. The last thing she cared about was a wet dress.

* * *

Downstairs, I attempted to get a few more dances before closing. Unfortunately, the Alpha-Strippers had decided to work on this particular evening. The Alpha-Strippers were a group of pompous, seldom-seen, surgically enhanced borgs, so nicknamed because of their undeniable earning power. The Alphas only needed to work one day a week to maintain their fortunes, and they seemed to always arrive en masse, phony breasts spilling cockeyed out of overpriced costumes, Vuitton handbags swinging. They clustered around the bar and cooed half-jokingly about which one of them would fuck the DJ that night. I wasn't going to make any money with all that premium poontang hovering around.

Dejected, I went back upstairs to sulk by the hot tub. But all that remained of Joni was her tracks, dainty wet footprints fading on the tile floor.

Good-bye, Yellow
Brick Road

By July, I was working sixty hours a week at the agency, doggedly trying to amass credit in the straight world. I almost believed I could abandon the disorderly chrysalis of my early twenties and emerge a sticky butterfly with a crash-proof flight plan. No dice; I was flailing. I was mistake-prone to begin with, and sleep deprivation didn't exactly complement my work performance. I kept a dilapidated pile of file folders on my desk in an attempt to look like I had a system, but the important documents I was meant to organize were as scrambled as my synapses. My paper trail had expanded into a four-lane highway, and I was royally fucked.

"You'll figure it out," my boss insisted when I approached her and voiced my concerns. "It's really not that hard to be a project manager."

Perhaps not for normal, hardworking folks, the kind who don't flash their genitals for pocket change. I, however, was overwhelmed by responsibility. Meanwhile, I couldn't stop thinking about stripping. Whenever I closed my eyes, I saw that familiar dizzying image of the eternal army of strippers traipsing down the spiral staircase, ghostly blondes, spectral redheads, grim and efficient in their descent to nowhere. Where were they going? Hell? Dillard's? The welfare office?

"You're lacking amino acids," Jonny declared when I told him that I couldn't concentrate at work. So we went to one of those musclehead health emporiums where they stock legal steroids by the bucket, and bought some L-tyrosine and ginseng supplements. I even popped some OTC trucker speed, hoping I'd turn into one of those hyperorganized junkies who can't stop cleaning. Nothing worked. I realized that I had to buckle down. Grow up. Put my aquiline nose to the corporate grindstone. Quit stripping, at least for the time being.

* * *

Like the craven wuss I am, I feared being sighted by the Mustaches when I hauled my stripperly belongings out of Big Pink. I crept into the building during the Saturday afternoon shift and hoped no one would notice me dumping out my locker into an army-surplus backpack. As I crossed the main floor to the elevator, I noticed that a weird, David Lynch-ian atmosphere pervaded the day shift. A walleyed girl in a red bridesmaid dress paced around onstage to jazz music while a deaf customer sat nearby and held up a sign that said TAKE OFF YR PANTY. The day manager, a ginger-haired linebacker of a woman, eyed me suspiciously but didn't say a word.

Once upstairs in the dressing room, I jimmied my locker open and grimaced at the junk I had amassed over a few months. The locker contained:

- One bottle of Wet 'n' Wild nail lacquer in Ruby Begonia (dark polish colors are ideal for lazy girls and Goths; they can be applied in endless sloppy coats, and cover hangnails and other neurotic excorciations).

- A brush with a Tribble-esque pouf of blonde wig hair ensnared in its bristles.

- Two black thongs in need of washing (and, possibly, disposal in a sealed biohazard receptacle).

- A carelessly opened package of bone-dry Huggies wipes.

- A pair of new-ish platforms that were retired when they battered my feet into a veritable Badlands of red and purple blisters.

- Assorted soiled dancewear items, one of them bearing a mysterious cloudy stain. (Russian dressing? *Hyuk!*)

- An extremely offensive foot funk, kind of like aged Camembert crossed with mink urea.

I threw on my backpack and hopped into the groaning elevator, riding downstairs with a pair of mute newbies in matching fluorescent coochie-cutters. They stared at me hollowly like the butchered twin girls in *The Shining*. I smiled at them, relieved to be escaping from the killing floor of Big Pink.

Jonny greeted me outside and we high-fived like accomplices in a jailbreak. Just then, one of my sky-high platform shoes fell out of my backpack onto the sidewalk as a couple walked past us arm-in-arm. The female half of the couple paused, looked at the fallen shoe, glanced up at the neon Deja Vu signage, then stared at me witheringly. She might as well have hissed *Stripper!* and lobbed a rock at my head. I grinned back sheepishly. Now that I was temporarily out of the game, I felt wholesome. Reconstructed. Like my forehead had been anointed with chrism, albeit briefly, and I had earned my wings (noble, seraphic wings, not the sparkling, marabou-trimmed kind that strippers named Angel sometimes wear).

"I think you were just outed," Jonny commented, picking the shoe up off the sidewalk and stuffing it back into my gaping bag.

"No one must know of the stripping!" I shouted jokingly, but my declaration had the acrid undertaste of truth. I hadn't told my family or even the lion's share of my friends about my buck-naked misadventure. I had a feeling it wasn't over yet.

Burnt Wienie Sandwich

August in Minneapolis: tattooed skin, outboard motors and summer hours. The city perspires Grain Belt beer, and its pale, bloated denizens bike shirtless and float like Wonder Bread on the lake off Hidden Beach. I found these civilian displays of nudity endearing, especially after months spent watching trim, tanned mutants dropping their panties for spare change.

Now that I had officially dropped my gig at Deja Vu, I was experiencing the sort of flat emotional state that serves as the perfect canvas for adventure. I decided to seize the malaise, so to speak, and work at an unfamiliar strip club for one night only. I figured I'd make a little mad money, get my rocks off and satisfy my anthropological yearnings. I wouldn't be satisfied until I'd investigated every local strip club from deep inside.

It was a Friday evening, and I had just gotten off work. I headed on foot from the agency to the warehouse district, carrying a Lund's grocery bag stuffed with costumes.

There were a handful of clubs in the area (Deja Vu, Choice, Dreamgirls, 418 and Augie's) but Dreamgirls intrigued me the most. The club was housed in a mostly abandoned building with a peeling black facade and an inexplicable mural of King Kong on the exposed wall. The lighted sign was a lewd Atlantic City relic shaped like an ejaculatory fountain flanked by palms, and the entrance was marked with a blue awning lined with chaser bulbs that had lost the thrill of the chase. From the outside, the place looked like a run-down jack shack*, a dollhouse so condemned I could already smell the dynamite. So of course, being a glutton for the grotesque, I felt compelled to take a peek.

As I approached the club, I saw that the facade of the building was obscured by scaffolding due to the construction of a new light-rail station. As a conciliatory measure toward inconvenienced customers, they had posted a large banner: DREAMGIRLS 'LIGHT RAIL INCONVENIENCE PARTY.' FREE COVER, FREE HOT DOGS, BEAUTIFUL LADIES. (You mean I'm going to be billed *beneath* the hot dogs? I'm in!)

Weiners notwithstanding, I knew the "free cover" part of the bargain was potentially lucrative. There were bound to be loads of turgid tightwads at the club if the entry fee was waived, and a Friday was likely to be busy anyway. My decision was made. I edged past the scaffolding and into Dreamgirls.

---

* *Jack shack*: noun, a strip club where hand jobs and other sexual acts are freely sold

Inside, a girl wearing a *Hustler* half-shirt and a dour expression was inflating balloons with a helium tank. Dreamgirls was a fully nude, nonalcoholic club, with standard dancing upstairs and a peep show called the Annex in the basement. From the front door, though, all I could see was a cramped vestibule and a bobbing murder of black balloons.

"Here to work tonight?" the doorman asked immediately, noticing my bag of costumes and synthetic hair.

"Can I?" I asked. "I've never worked here before."

"No problem," he said. "Just let me see some identification." I handed over my nearly expired driver's license (me exactly four years earlier, a fresh-faced college student ideologically opposed to the sex industry).

"Looks good," he said. "You can change upstairs."

The locker room was Mildew Fest Midwest, with broken lockers hanging agape to reveal costumes, cosmetics organizers and damp towels. Still, there was plenty of counter space to stake out, which I appreciated. I pulled out my wig and began detangling it with my fingers. Since the day shift was still winding down and night girls are customarily late for work, the dressing room was empty.

Two cheerful day girls came in and introduced themselves. Their names were Zoey and Frankie. Zoey wore a red Farrah wig ("I've got a blue mohawk underneath," she confessed). Frankie was a gangly sweetheart with Becky Thatcher freckles and dear skinny legs.

"Get dressed and we'll show you around," Frankie offered.

"You're hot. We like you," Zoey elaborated.

I kicked off my clogs, apologized for my chronic foot

stink and quickly changed into my zebra-print slip dress, pink platform shoes and mangled wig.

"Want to see the Annex?" Zoey asked me. I did.

* * *

The Annex operated independently of the action upstairs. As the three of us rode the wheezing elevator down to the bowels of the club, Frankie and Zoey explained the concept: The Annex consisted of one-on-one erotic booth shows, where customers could jerk off behind Plexiglas while interacting with their stripper of choice. Frankie and Zoey told me they worked in the Annex frequently.

"What do you do in there?" I asked.

"Well, I usually just get naked and masturbate. I won't finger myself if I think it's a cop, though. It's illegal to stick anything in there," Zoey said.

"Zoey and I did a girl-girl show earlier today," Frankie offered. "It was really hard not to laugh, because the guy had an enormous cock." She spanned her hands wide, indicating a purple monster. "I mean, it was *huge!*"

"We pretended to go down on each other," Zoey said, flicking her tongue to illustrate. "It was weird."

"I was all like, 'Oh, mister, your cock is so big!'" Frankie said. "We were dying."

"He squirted cum all over the glass, and I was like, *I can't look!*" Zoey marveled. "We both closed our eyes."

The girls showed me the themed booths, which included a mock dungeon with hanging chains and a "Water Fantasy" booth complete with working shower. (For some reason, I found it amusing that there was a cake of soap and a nearly depleted bottle of Herbal Essences on the floor; what commitment to realism!) Frankie explained that the private shows cost a minimum of ten dollars, and that the girl could charge whatever she wanted in addition.

"Can I just work down here all night?" I asked. The prospect was so foul I couldn't resist. I'd gone over the edge in my quest to see how the naked half lived.

"Well, usually we snag guys upstairs and bring them down here if they want a private show," Frankie explained.

"How is it upstairs, anyway?" I asked.

"Sometimes it's busy, sometimes it's not." Zoey shrugged. "I'm not making much lately."

I had high hopes for tonight's head count; after all, who could resist free hot dogs? Surely Dreamgirls would be overrun by wealthy, monocle-twirling dukes pressing rare Tahitian pearls into our palms. This was bound to be the classiest night of adult entertainment Minneapolis had ever seen, and I was determined to attend the ball. I excused myself politely, and rode back up to the first floor. The smell of salted meat drifted down the elevator shaft: *The hot dogs had entered the building.*

* * *

My first glance of the club's main room was disorienting. Dreamgirls was like Deja Vu's dimmer fraternal twin, right down to the pattern on the carpet and the layout of the stage. Mirrored ceilings created the illusion of Bosch-like orgiastic chaos in a relatively small room. Fat dark couches lined the walls like biopsied moles. I shivered in my sheer dress; the air conditioning was evidently set to zero degrees Kelvin.

An older man sauntered over and eyed me from head to toe. "God bless America!" he declared appreciatively.

"Hi," I said, smiling. "I'm Cherish."

"How about a bed dance?" he asked, throwing his arm around my shoulders.

"Absolutely!" I said, steeling myself for a nine-minute cock tease. On one hand, bed dances made me want to retch. On the other hand, sixty clams could buy a lot of Zappa records and vodka Cokes.

He laughed. "I'm kidding. I'm the owner. Have you ever danced before?"

I reddened. "Yeah, at Deja Vu."

"I own that club, too," he said. That explained the familiar decor. It occurred to me that this man was the primary beneficiary of all the outrageous house fees I'd paid. He was probably disgustingly rich, with a zero-depth pool and a home gym and all that *MTV Cribs* shit. I wanted to punch him, or better yet, force him to spend the evening naked and groveling for tips.

"Cool," I lied. "I love the Vu."

"This place works the same way," the owner said. "Twenty for dances, sixty for beds. Good luck tonight."

"I appreciate it," I said. Nearby, a waitress in the requisite miniskirt and sneakers leaned over a steam tray and doled out hot dogs with tongs.

* * *

As the clock neared seven, more strippers emerged from the dressing room in their sparkling tatters and towering footwear. While there were a few standard-issue photo negatives (platinum blondes with deep tans, steeped in body), most of the girls were tattooed punk chicks, sepulchral Goths with fishhook piercings, fat cheerleaders and assorted misfits straight out of the "Alternative Lifestyles" column in the local weekly. Refreshing.

One of the girls introduced herself to me immediately, and revealed that it was her first night at Dreamgirls. Leela was eighteen years old, wearing a steel bull ring through her septum and tangled hair extensions. Her lips were painted as black as freshly laid asphalt.

"I just got a drum kit," she told me. "I'm so excited! Me and my friends are going to start a punk band."

"I play bass," I said, feeling hopelessly square in my blonde wig.

"We should jam sometime!" Leela exclaimed.

"I'm twenty-five," I said. "I'm old enough to be your math tutor."

Leela's mouth formed a black-lipsticked O. "You don't look that old!"

"I guess I'm well preserved," I said.

Since the stage was still vacant, Leela and I went up to practice pole tricks. She was as nimble as the howler monkeys at the Como Zoo; I was my usual unwieldy self.

"This one is easy," Leela said breathlessly, showing me a rapid inverted maneuver. "Try it."

I tried, and wound up tangled on the floor. "Not a

chance, honey. I've never been much of a pole-lympian."
A special pole-lympian, perhaps.

"But it's easy!" Leela insisted, clinging to the pole
somewhere above my head. She flipped upside down, exposing the rows of infinitesimal braids that attached her
hair extensions to her scalp.

"Must be my rheumatoid arthritis acting up," I said.

* * *

A cute Asian girl strolled up to me with a broad, menacing
smile on her face and next to nothing on her little brown
body. She had eschewed the usual stilettos in favor of well-
worn sandals, but somehow this bohemian faux pas worked
in her favor. She seized my tits and squeezed them approvingly. Then I felt her hand slip down the front of my
thong along with something cool and papery. She pressed
a dollar bill against my pussy, withdrew her now-empty
hand, giggled at her own audacity and walked away without
saying a word.

"Thanks for the dollar," I called after her.

"See, you're not that bad," Leela said. "Nikita likes
you."

* * *

The stage rotation began. I had requested Aerosmith from
the DJ, and to my delight, he chose the song "Pink" from
their extensive catalog. "Pink," in my opinion, is one of
the most appropriate songs for a girl working without
pants. After all, isn't pink what it's all about at the juice

bars? I stripped down to my birthday suit, lay down on-stage and spread like Hellmann's. My pussy isn't a tucked, tidy clover like some girls have; in fact, it's not even pink. I have a dark, sinister-looking taco lengua, more bruised than blushing. But I learned early on that no one cares what you've got between your legs. Sloppy, tight, pierced, shaved, underaged or "distinguished," it's still pussy and it's worth its depth in molten gold when you're a stripper.

Onstage acrobatics notwithstanding, the room was positively dead. The crowd was sparse for any night, let alone a Friday. Deja Vu was packed wall-to-wall with drunk collegiate types on weekends; it seemed strange that a club that was nearly identical couldn't seem to attract customers. And yet I could see why people avoided Dreamgirls. It was more like Night Terror Girls, a colossal dump, a sick building. Money had obviously been poured into the club, but there was an unmistakable vibe of creeping disrepair. Even the paid feature dancer, an enamel-hard blonde in pleather chaps, puckered miserably in a corner. The innately depressing presence of processed meat didn't help matters.

After an hour or two, I couldn't seem to get any lap dances, so I sat down with Leela to watch the stage show for a while. One of the dancers had an ornate tattoo inked across the back of her shoulders that read "Lost Girl." I'd seen a lot of body art in my time stripping, everything from wicked pixies to cannabis leaves to blurred, brutal prison tattoos of boyfriends' names. But I'd never seen anything quite so striking as "Lost Girl." It was like a life story in two words.

The lost girl led the pack when we took the stage en masse for the standard bachelor hazing. We formed the usual staggered V, and the bored bachelor assumed the position. (I happily noted that Dreamgirls didn't use "We Want Some Pussy" as the accompaniment for this ritual, though the DJ had selected a suitably vulgar porn-rap classic.) Leela climbed the pole and straddled the bachelor's face, legs outstretched. She was setting herself up for a "teeter-totter," a popular bachelor-torturing move in which two girls face each other on the pole and hump the guy's face in a rhythmic seesaw motion.

She gestured to me. "C'mon, Cherish, do a teeter-totter with me!"

I groaned and sat down on the stage. "I'll pass." I was in a stormy mood. At this point, I'd barely cleared my house fee and my drink hustle was nil.

Someone else seized the teeter-totter opportunity, and she and Leela merrily bobbed back and forth in the face of ennui.

* * *

If Schieks, with its crystal and Cristal, was cinematic, then Dreamgirls was cinema verité. Every little girl in the place was wearing a frown. I gave a few lap dances, but the customers were reluctant to part with their money. (I should have known a bunch of hot dog freeloaders would be loathe to spend their unemployment checks on prick-teasers.) I sat with a stoic Sudanese man for a while, but he was more interested in pawing my breasts and asking me to fuck him than paying for any legal favors.

"Outside?" he asked like a skipping record. "How much to sex me outside?"

"Sorry, I don't do that," I said, an apologetic-yet-murderous smile pasted on my face. I used a syrupy, pedantic tone of voice whenever I chastised foreigners for soliciting sex. It happened at least three times nightly, so I was accustomed to it.

"*Whyyyy?*" he asked. (An agonized "why" was always phase two of the "Clever Foreigner Sex Push.")

"Because it's illegal, and because I don't want to," I replied, knowing he'd offer me $100 next.

"Oh, come on. Hundred dollar," he insisted. Phase three, dead on as always.

"No," I said. "Sorry." I disengaged myself and walked away. My feet throbbed like the graphic in an aspirin commercial. There was no Jacuzzi at Dreamgirls, though, so I had nowhere to soak my dogs. I thought I might be able to find an unoccupied toilet, but the lone commode I'd seen looked rather unappealing.

"How's your night going?" Leela asked me glumly.

"Horrendous," I said. "How about you?"

"I've only gotten one dance," she said, her pierced lower lip drooping in defeat. "This place sucks."

"I wonder if it's always this bad?" I asked.

"I heard it was," Leela said. "I only came here because I got fired from Choice."

"How did that happen?" Getting fired from a nudie bar requires an act of theft or homicide, so I was curious how a cheerful peewee like Leela had gotten herself shitcanned.

"Some girl lied and said I punched her in the face," Leela said disdainfully.

"Would you go back to Choice if you could?" I asked.

"Oh yeah," Leela brightened. "I did all right there. Once I gave thirty consecutive lap dances to a major league hockey player. My wig fell off during the seventeenth dance, and he was like, 'Keep going! I don't care!' It was the most money I ever made in one night."

"I keep hearing about strippers having encounters with athletes," I mused.

"It'll happen to you eventually, if you stick around," Leela said.*

By four a.m., the club was empty and the dressing room was packed with dejected girls with swollen feet. There was that usual bracing aura after a long weekend night fueled by Red Bull and blow: people talking too loud, girls flinging eyeliner pencils at each other, florid declarations of lust/rage/poverty.

One dancer caught my attention. She was one of the skinniest people I'd ever seen, but it wasn't a privileged kind of skinny. Her acne-ravaged face had been troweled over with Pan-Cake makeup; her hairpiece was a dull Daniel Boone pelt. She stood in the middle of the dressing room, frankly naked. Her breasts reminded me of the slack teats I'd gawked at in *National Geographic* as a kid.

---

* It did happen. I gave exactly two dances to one of the Minnesota Vikings, and he was wearing these wretched spandex pants, accessoried with a stylish boner. He didn't even buy me a Coke.

"You always think you're gonna love your kid's dad *forevvver*," she drawled. " 'Cause that's your baby's *daaaddy*. You kin't let go, no matter how hard you try."

"It's true," a girl said. "But I don't want nothing else from Bill but forty dollars a week."

"Your baby's *daaaddy*," the skinny one repeated, smiling broadly at some private remembrance. "You think it's gonna be forever, but it ain't."

* * *

The dancers filed downstairs. The closing procedure was the same as at Deja Vu (a brief pep talk, followed by payout) but with an intriguing twist: The manager was a raving, racist wingnut on the brink of cardiac arrest.

"*You stupid broke-ass bitches!*" he shouted as we sat motionless on the soiled couches. "Stupid fat sluts! No wonder we can't get any people in this bitch!"*

At that moment, several black girls crept down from the dressing room. "Well, well," the manager sputtered, noticing them. "If it isn't the three little niggers! How much did you bitches make off the homos tonight?"

The girls rolled their eyes in disgust and joined the rest of the dancers on the soiled couches.

"I watch you drunk bitches," the manager warned. "I see you sneaking booze and drugs. *Treena.*" He pointed at a girl who I assumed was Treena. She giggled, seemingly

---

* This quickly became a humorous catchphrase in the Jonny-Diablo household. "We need some groceries in this bitch!"

unfazed by his vitriol. I sensed that hate speech was a nightly tradition at Dreamgirls.

"I'd better see every girl sitting with a homo next time," the manager continued. "I'd better not see any of you up in the dressing room, sitting on your fat asses and drinking and complaining about how you can't make any money."

The girls nodded. I wondered why the obviously het-ero patrons of the club had been dubbed "homos" by the manager, but I decided it was best not to ask.

"All right, let's get this over with," the manager con-cluded, and sat down to collect his take as the chastised girls dutifully formed a single-file line, cash in hand.

When it was my turn to pay the house, I approached the manager with trepidation. Shockingly, he was the very picture of gentility, smiling at me like a kindly uncle.

"Are you going to work with us again, sweetheart?" he asked, palming the skimpy five-dollar tip I was loathe to part with but scared to withhold.

"I think so," I fibbed, desperate to leave as quickly as possible.

"Well," he said, "we'd love to have you back."

Hot dog!

The Ten Worst Songs to Strip To

1. That Midnight Oil song about aborigines.

2. "Friday I'm in Love" by the Cure. Robert Smith's maudlin gasping is ideal for weekends spent sobbing outside your ex-husband's duplex, but utterly destructive to a hot stage set.

3. "Hey Ya" by Outkast. This is a song everyone loves ('cause it's admittedly super sick), but the average stripper needs to toot an eightball to keep up with those psycho beats. Besides, no one wants to be reminded of marital strife while your ass is in their face.

4. "Ice Ice Baby" by Vanilla Ice. Widely used as "punishment" by passive-aggressive DJs who are irritated with a specific stripper for undertipping.

5. "Girls" by the Beastie Boys. While this is a popular juke selection with the leering, cunt-hating jamoches who frequent strip clubs, those xylophones inevitably kill the mood.

6. Anything by Britney Spears. Chances are, you'll piss off a veteran stripper at your club who staked a permanent claim on the Britney catalog back in 1998, and who has tightly choreographed stage sets for every Brit-

ney song (even "Don't Let Me Be the Last to Know"). Admit defeat.

7. Any Eminem song about matricide, Quaaludes or fatherhood.

8. "Elenore" by the Turtles. I know you adore this twee follow-up hit from those sixties Los Angeles scenesters, but *resist!*

9. "Hotel California" by the crappy post-country incarnation of the Eagles. You'll make everyone angry. All strippers hate Joe Walsh; I don't know why.

10. "The More You Ignore Me, The Closer I Get" by Morrissey. Encourages stalkers, and the last thing you want is Freddy the Reg showing up at your day job with a bundle of dyed carnations and a loaded .45.

Rawhide

At the close of August, Jonny and I fueled up the Pussy Wagon (so named because I'd paid for it with miles of horizontal smiles) and hauled ass out West. It was our first road trip as a couple, and it was just as idyllic and color-saturated as I'd imagined; all quirky landmarks and gunfight reenactments and sunsets pooling like abandoned Creamsicles on the rugged horizon. We went to the night rodeo in Cody, Wyoming, where an incongruous Brazilian clown made me think of Joni, the pregnant maid. We chowed on "prairie oysters," otherwise known as deep-fried bull testicles, in a cowboy bar (I snapped photos of Jonny gamely choking down the balls while the windburnt locals looked on in rheumy-eyed amusement). We went to every monument, museum and buckskin-laden gift shop we could fingerpoint in the Frommer's. We drove to Yellowstone, Medicine Wheel and Mount Rushmore.

I had a predictable epiphany out West as well. (Who could avoid an epiphany when surrounded by awe-inspiring vistas and $4.95 prime rib specials?) Anyway, I realized that it wasn't stripping that had made me feel uneasy of late. Sure, Deja Vu was a depressing, poorly managed, black, black suckhole, but what had genuinely bummed me out was the fact that I'd *failed*. Flunked. I'd been a sorry excuse for a stripper, two thousand light-years from the self-possessed, pole-polishing goddess I'd envisioned myself becoming. I'd earned shit because I'd felt like shit. I'd hauled years of geek-damage and self-loathing around that club like a dromedary's hump; no wonder guys waved me away like a stink. Most egregious of all, I'd allowed myself to be totally exploited by customers because I couldn't imagine why anyone would want me otherwise. I'd offered my ass up at a discount. In marketing parlance, I'd never created a demand.

Meanwhile, my new gig at the agency had netted me nothing but a nickel-and-dime raise and a nascent peptic ulcer that made me bleed from my ass. I'd never been an organized person, so what had compelled me to accept a promotion that involved creating order from other people's chaos? I suspected that I'd quit the wrong job, and I told Jonny so as I cruised through the Bighorn Mountains at a joyfully idiotic seventy miles per hour.

"I think you're right," Jonny said, surprising me. "You don't seem to be through with stripping, really."

"I'm through with stripping," I said. "Stripping isn't through with me. You know how I inexplicably did that

Dreamgirls thing last month? What was that? Why can't I stop taking my clothes off in dive clubs? There must be a reason."

"Are you thinking about 'going pro'?" Jonny asked. "Like, quitting your day job and stripping full-time at a new club?"

"I know it sounds like madness," I said. "But the agency is driving me batshit, and I haven't wrung nearly enough money out of the sex industry."

"Then do it," Jonny said. "Quit."

"I've never not had a real job," I mused, gripping the steering wheel as we roared past a runaway truck lane.

*　*　*

I was aware that my family and friends saw my job at the advertising agency as a plum gig. After all, I was lucky to be working in a progressive environment where creative trendoids vastly outnumbered bean counters. (Never mind the fact that my job accounted to being a human sorting mechanism, or that a "forthcoming" raise had been delayed for months.) My modicum of success at the agency meant nothing to me; it wasn't an indicator of my worth as a person. Whereas a single good night of stripping could elevate my sense of self to Kilimanjaro altitudes. That was real approval, the assurance that Me the Brand was fit for sale. No middle manager could accurately put a price on my intellect or work ethic, but I knew precisely how much my body was worth per pound on any given night in the all-girl charcuterie. This concrete information was reassuring, much more so than the bogus corporate praise I'd garnered in the past.

I left my job at the agency almost instantly upon returning from the trip. Quitting turned out to be a tepid 2.5 on the dropped-bombshell impact scale. My boss was fairly nonchalant about the announcement, imperceptibly pursing her flawlessly lipsticked puss (*Don't mess your MAC Spice, honey*). "I sensed you weren't happy with the position," she sighed as I stood red-faced in her immaculate, suburban-Zen cubicle. "Good luck."

A farewell ice-cream social was hastily arranged. (All I remember about it was that all the guys gorged themselves on chocolate-chocolate chip while my female coworkers nibbled cautiously on lemon sorbet.) I lied my way through the exit interview ("I'm going to herbal cosmetology school!") and was presently released from my duties with naught but a song in my heart and a knapsack full of stolen office supplies.

Doll Parts

Working at a nude hustle club had emboldened me. I was fearless, jaded and calloused from the waist down. My wallet was thin, my boundaries ambiguous. I was ready to transition from dancing girl to peep-show prisoner, and I knew just the place to do it.

Sex World is a three-story, twenty-four-hour circus-themed porn emporium featuring "live" nude models (as opposed to comely zombies?), video booths, smoking paraphernalia and every imaginable sexual novelty from dick-shaped lollies to cyberjelly replicas of porn star Alisha Klass's anal cavity. Snickering bachelorettes share the aisles with fidgeting perverts, and the joint is perpetually jumpin'—where else can one procure an erotic cake (breasts and cocks artlessly rendered in frigid buttercream), a three-foot bong and a stash of amateur porn all under one roof? It's the Wal-Mart of sex, the kind of place where you go simply to purchase the latest issue of

Taboo and wind up buying four vibrators and T.T. Boy's entire oeuvre on VHS.

The peep show at Sex World, otherwise known as "the Dollhouse," was notorious for the fact that the girls in its employ were on public display. They lounged behind a pane of glass like Barbies with giantism, fully visible to the flesh-starved crowds that milled in and out of the store at literally all hours. When a customer wanted a show, he'd point dumbly to the girl he liked the best, and she'd join him in one of the private booths along the east wall of the enclosure. I'd shopped at Sex World before, but I'd never approached the window; it seemed like a disturbingly concrete point of demarcation between "us" and "them," and I didn't want to spook the fish. Plus, the peep-show girls looked so hip hanging out and smoking in their little Amsterdam, and I was afraid if I walked up and perused their environment they might poke fun at me. (I know, I'm a total wienie.)

After the hard hustle of working the clubs downtown, the prospect of working at the Dollhouse was tempting indeed. I viewed it as a sex-work sabbatical, a chance to relax in a glass box for a while and let the customers solicit me before returning to the hectic stripping scene. I'd heard that Sex World issued weekly paychecks and offered health benefits, which had serious appeal compared to the independent-contractor status most strip clubs offered (along with an extremely broad interpretation of the "independent" part). I decided to apply and see if I'd be asked to join the ranks of the dolls.

After filling out a standard application (under "Military Rankings" I wrote "Major Babe"), I posed for a fully clothed Polaroid taken by a sullen clerk with wooden plugs corking his stretched earlobes. Within a couple of days, I received a call from the peep-show manager, a self-aggrandizing Don King of a woman who looked like she'd both weathered and administered beatings. She always referred to her employees as "the dolls," matter-of-factly and without affection.

"One of the dolls just quit, so I have a shift open from six to midnight," she told me. "Five days a week. Take it or leave it." I took it.

"Okay. Bring a blanket, some lube and whatever sex toys you want to use," she added. "These are masturbation shows, and you'll make the most money if you use toys."

I agreed, but I neglected to ask if I'd be able to see every Tom, Dick and Harry as they tooled like Bonobo monkeys on the opposite side of the booth. For some reason, the voyeuristic aspect of the gig, what *I* would see, concerned me most of all.

My first day in the Dollhouse was a Monday. The manager showed me how to get inside via an ingenious secret entrance (an obvious portal to Doll-land would have attracted too many potential rapists/lovelorn perverts). She led me down a narrow hallway to the dressing area, which was so tiny it made the locker room at the Skyway Lounge look like backstage at the Tropicana. There was a sink, a punch clock, a coffeemaker and not much else. Across from the dressing room were three doors marked A, B and C. These were the entrances to the cramped booths where the shows were done. I was told to pick a booth to work in. I chose A. It was painted pink on the inside, and contained a cracked leatherette chaise with brackish stuffing issuing from the seams. There was a portable CD player tethered to the wall with an imposingly large chain; I guessed they took theft seriously at the Dollhouse. A long, thick pane of two-way glass separated my side of the booth from the customer's side (so I *would* have to look at all those masturbating plumbers, lawyers and COBOL programmers after all!), and both sides had one of those black prison phones to enable filthy communiqués.

Around the corner was the so-called den, the display area where the girls hung out in full view of the store until they were summoned for a show. (Most people I knew called it "the box," as in, "You mean you're one of those girls in the box at Sex World?!") The den was painted oxblood red with a splishy gold faux finish. There was a red sofa shaped like Marilyn's pucker, and a pair of chairs shaped like stiletto heels. It was all very reminiscent of the eighties trend toward "wacky" high-concept furniture; I half-expected to see a hamburger phone. There were a few dated issues of *Entertainment Weekly* strewn about, and the room smelled like recent Chinese takeout. A girl in a dark pageboy wig sat on the couch with a sketchbook and a tin of pastels in her lap; she smiled and introduced herself as MacKenzie.

Harsh fluorescent light fixtures surrounded the front display window. Compared to the ambient subterranean darkness of strip clubs, this grocery store lighting was *molto* unflattering, especially considering I'd be displayed like a veal chop for all to see. I noticed a boldly printed note taped beneath the window. A transcript of the memo, punctuation and spelling preserved:

> TO WHOM IT MAY CONCERN I WANT THESE LIGHTS
> ON ALL THE TIME I DON'T CARE HOW THEY MAKE
> YOU LOOK OR IF YOUR GETTING A HEADACHE IF
> I FIND THEM TURNED OFF YOULL RECIVE A
> WRITTEN WARNING AND OH YES I WILL WRITE
> YOU UP FOR SOME DUMD SHIT LIKE THE LIGHTS
> NOT BEING ON TRY ME ANY QUESTIONS.

I was a long way from those scooter-riding copywriters at the ad agency.

Another notable feature of the den was the two-way radios. The peep-show girls had a pair for security reasons, but the cashiers and sales help throughout the vast Sex World complex used them to ask each other questions when a customer made a specific inquiry. I instantly knew I'd enjoy eavesdropping on the clerks' conversations. As I unpacked my leopard-print blanket and nubby pink vibrator, I overheard the following exchange on the radio:

Clerk #1: "What's that movie called with the people having sex underwater?"

Clerk #2: "Either *Sex Underwater* or *Underwater Sex.*"

Clerk #1: "Roger that."

I draped the chaise in my booth with the blanket (the last thing I wanted to do was frolic in some other girl's residual sticky-icky) and placed my vibrator on the window ledge. When I peeked into MacKenzie's booth, I noticed that she'd brought a huge Tupperware container that was literally overflowing with tools of the trade. There were jelly dongs of all lengths, girths and skin tones, anal plugs, nipple clamps, ben-wa balls, a flog, a can of whipped cream and even a so-called "window rider" (a dildo that could be mounted on the glass with a suction cup and gaily fucked by a flexible girl). I suddenly felt a wave of inadequacy due to my wee pink gherkin of a vibrator. Penis-proxy envy.

The manager left, and MacKenzie explained to me that a receipt printed each time a customer deposited money in the booth. We were to turn in our receipts at the end of each night, and each Friday we'd receive a check for half the sum of our receipt totals. The store kept the other half, which seemed excessive, but I was accustomed to being swindled by the flesh trade by then.

I crept into the dressing room and donned an eight-dollar nautical bikini from Hot Topic, stilettos and a new black Mia Wallace wig. I didn't want any of the jerks from Deja Vu to come over and heckle me, so I'd reinvented myself as a Goth pinup. I joined MacKenzie in the den; we sat in silence and waited for customers desirous of ass to tap the glass. I wondered what my first show would be like, and if it would be revolting to watch a strange guy masturbate to completion. Finally, a guy who looked like Bill Gates walked up and pointed to me mutely. Showtime!

When we were settled in our respective sides of the booth, Bill Gates picked up the prison phone and re-

quested a forty-dollar nude show. I promptly took off my
bikini and began awkwardly preening and fondling myself
like a drunk socialite at a photo op. (I've always been a
fairly no-nonsense masturbator, and I wasn't quite sure
how to glamorize the act for public consumption.)

To my confusion, Bill Gates began removing all his
clothes, hanging them slowly and methodically on a hook
that had been provided on his side of the booth. When he
was completely naked, he grinned at me, produced an
extra-large bottle of Astroglide, poured an utterly excessive amount into his palm, sat down and began fingering
his asshole contentedly. *Squelch, squelch, squelch.*

I gulped and continued to masturbate. Bill gestured
for me to insert a couple of fingers into my pussy, so I
did. The rules about penetration were very specific at the
Dollhouse. Technically, inserting fingers or toys was illegal, but vaginal and anal toy shows comprised most of our
business. To circumvent this hurdle, we were instructed
to never insert anything anywhere until the customer was
masturbating. The logic behind this was that an under-
cover cop on duty was unlikely to drop his pants and jack
off. Therefore, it was safe to proceed with a toy show once
the customer had whipped out his rig. This was neatly
summed up on an amusing sign posted in each booth: IF
YOU DON'T SEE SKIN-ON-SKIN, DON'T YOU PUT NOTH-
ING IN!

When Bill Gates came, he motioned for me to put my
head up near the glass, affording me a clinical perspective
of his orgasm. Rather than the mighty geyser of baby-gravy

I'd feared, it was a disappointing trickle of ejaculate, clear and sticky like albumen. I suspected he'd already masturbated earlier in the day. Still, I stared up at him with fake reverence, as if he'd gifted me with the display of a lifetime. *Mount St. Helens, eat your molten heart out!* I left the booth and washed my hands aggressively at the sink. MacKenzie coughed drily in the den, and I wondered if it was embarrassing knowing that your coworker had just been masturbating several feet away. If it was, I suspected I'd have to get over it quickly.

* * *

During my first night, I serviced the following customers:

1. A shoe freak who begged me to lick one of my stilettos whilst "jacking off" the heel of the other. He told me I was a natural at jacking off shoes. (Frankly, I had no idea.) In a successful attempt to hasten his orgasm, I cooed, "Ooh, I wish you could cum on my shoes." He replied, "Really? Want my phone number?" *Nein.*

2. An immaculately dressed businessman whose wife had ordered him to go to Sex World, get a peep-show girl to masturbate and describe the entire thing to her via cell phone while *she* masturbated. To my relief, he was fairly complimentary in his description of my technique. He kept telling his wife, "No, seriously, she's quite attractive," as if

they'd both been expecting me to be a hatchet-faced leper.

3. A leering young man who told me that he frequently fucked his sister and that my pussy looked exactly like hers. I suggested she sneak in and cover a few shifts for me, à la *The Patty Duke Show,* since we'd be indistinguishable from the waist down. He was from Ecuador, though, so he didn't understand.

4. A guy who wanted to be dominated and said things like, "Fuck my ass! I'm your sissy maid!" provoking a very un-mistress-y gale of giggles on my side of the booth. (Bossy bottoms absolutely slay me.)

When my shift was over six hours later, I swabbed down the chaise and phone using alcohol and hospital-grade disinfectant as per the rules. The stink reminded me of a shopping mall ear-piercing kiosk. Luckily, the dolls weren't required to clean the "client side" of the booth. That task was reserved for a cadre of Goth janitors, one of whom wore a T-shirt that said SMOKE CRACK AND WORSHIP SATAN as he mopped up the man-made lagoon on the floor of my booth.

As I left the store and hailed a cab, I felt strangely satisfied. I'd made $200 for a laughably minimal amount of effort. I mean, I actually got paid to masturbate for six hours! Unlike at Deja Vu, there were no fines or mandatory tipouts to worry about. No soda-pop hustle or groping customers. I felt as if I was actually in control of my developing talent as a sexual surrogate. Behind the window, I felt cherished and untouchable, like a dildo-wielding *Precious Moments* tchotchke. Pristine. Like Snow White in her glass coffin, preserved for the masses.

* * *

After a week or so, I'd met or worked with just about everyone employed at the Dollhouse. There were around ten girls working at the peep show, usually two or three on each shift. They were physically diverse—some fat, some lanky, some glamorous stripper-types in expensive costumes, some welfare queens in bare feet and Baby Phat sweatpants. One of them, Ava, was seven months pregnant and could squeeze colostrum from her nipples, much to the delight of our mommy-fetishist customers. One of the "girls" was a former journalist of forty-two, though she could handily pass for thirty-something. Donna, our resident head case, was fond of slashing at her own flesh, and her pretty white arms were latticed with scabs. When she was stoned, she'd cackle maniacally like Tom Hulce in *Amadeus*. Another girl, Ariel, was undeniably gorgeous, but she was convinced she was fat and disgusting. She'd sit and compulsively smooth her thighs, talking in quiet, even tones about how every time she was passed over by a customer, she mentally added ten minutes to her daily workout regime.

(Ariel, for all her insecurities, had the loudest, most powerful vibrator in existence. I'm serious; this instrument of "pleasure" must have been of dubious legality. When she went into her booth for shows, it sounded like she was operating a leaf blower in there. I half expected the scent of scorched flesh to waft from her booth; that's how much friction this thing generated. But, she boasted, she couldn't come any other way.)

* * *

The manager always offered jobs to very young girls who applied. Once, she hired two teenage sisters who routinely and cheerfully offered to meet customers outside and fuck them in the parking lot after work. When someone complained to the manager that the new girls were using the peep show to hook up with potential johns, the manager replied, "White guys like young girls. They'll bring in money for the store. I can't fire them." The funny thing was that the sisters were hardly nubile, creamy-skinned Lolitas blushing on the bough. In fact, one of them looked like she'd beaten herself with a tire iron during a smallpox-induced hallucination, and the other looked like a close-up photo of a wolf spider. But the manager was so convinced of their youthful "appeal" that she kept the sisters on until they simply stopped showing up.

Girls turning tricks presented a criminal threat, but the manager was far more paranoid about drug use. There was a threatening sign posted at the peep show that read, NO DRUGS ARE ALLOWED AT WORK! THIS INCLUDES POT, ACID, HEROIN, COCAINE, HAPPY PILLS, PILLS WITH STUFF IN THEM, CRACK, AND ANY OTHER BULLSHIT UPPERS OR DOWNERS THAT YOU MAY BE CARRYING. I can't imagine a sign like that being posted in the break room at an H&R Block, you know? However, I found that while many of the strippers I knew had become champagne drunks out of necessity, very few of them were bona-freak junkies. I attribute this finding to core Minnesota decency, since I've heard many contrasting stories from other corners of these United States.

For instance, one girl I worked with was twenty-four, a prostitute and a mother of three. But she once told a story in the dressing room about discovering cocaine at an acquaintance's house: "I'd never seen cocaine in real life," she said earnestly. "But I saw the movie *Blow*, so I knew it was coke."

We all laughed good-naturedly at her naive conviction. It seemed so weird that a girl who regularly boinked complete strangers had only seen cocaine in the movies. The world of stripping is populated with such contradictions, suburban girls with bruised veins, ghetto girls on Atkins, innocents who strip to get dirty and dirty girls who strip to clean up. The whole scene is bananas.

* * *

The customers at Sex World were their own brand of bizarro. Foot-fucking, cross-dressing and sadomasochism were the most commonly cited fetishes, but loads of guys were into "golden showers" and other varieties of fun-by-the-fluid-ounce. Frequently, customers asked me to pee, or alternately, to sell them a cup of my urine. This was forbidden according to a posted memo that read, NO SHOWER SHOWS, AKA 'PEE SHOWS.' THOSE CAUGHT DOING SO WILL BE FIRED. However, a couple of girls had successfully sold their used tampons to customers, one of whom was willing to pay $50 to watch a girl ceremoniously extract a soiled Tampax from her person.

Sometimes I got bored with run-of-the-mill Plexiglas johns and the tired *Penthouse Forum* fantasies they absently mumbled into the phone. To combat ennui, I'd make up absurd stories that bordered on the avant-garde. For example, the following exchange occurred in my booth and was duly recorded:

Customer (whipping out standard-model short, pink Minnesota dick): "Hey, baby. How old are you?"

Your Writer: "Twenty."*

Customer: "So, tell me something sexy. Tell me about the first time you had sex."

YW: "I was, uh, at tennis camp.** I was only thirteen, and I had this really hot, overbearing tennis instructor who was, like, thirty-something. One day he decided to punish me for my sorry backhand, so he just *fucked* me. In the ass."

Customer (impressed): "You had anal your very first time?"

YW: "Anal and regular, yes. Then, he spanked my ass with a tennis racket." (*At this point, I accidentally allowed a snicker to es-*

---

* I was twenty-five.
** I've never been to tennis camp, nor am I familiar with the rules of tennis.

cape.) "Sorry. I was just remembering something funny that happened at camp."

Customer: "That's hot. What's the naughtiest thing you've ever done?"

YW: "Aside from the tennis camp incident? Well, I have a cousin who's only fourteen, and I fucked her recently."*

Customer: "Ohhhhh yeah."

YW: "She's, uh, an elite-level competitive rhythmic gymnast.** You know, those girls who jump around twirling a ribbon to 'A Fifth of Beethoven'? So she's really flexible and stuff. I told her I'd train her to be a lesbian, and then I fucked her with a big dildo. My family would be heartbroken if they knew."

Customer: "Was she shaved?"

YW: "She's way too naive to think of such a thing."

Customer: "How old were you when you fucked her?"

YW: "Nineteen, so it was, uh, last year?"

Customer: "So you're in college then?"

YW: "I went for a little while, but I dropped out."***

---

* No I didn't.
** Where do I get this stuff?
*** I graduated.

Customer (approaching orgasm): "What's the biggest cock you've ever had?"

YW: "Well . . . last year I was in a Hungarian porn film.* Actually, it was a series of three films, but none of them are available in the States. My male costar was . . . he was a count. A Hungarian count. Isn't that interesting, royalty starring in a porn movie? Anyway, he had a ten-inch cock."

Customer (ejaculating): "Blarrrgh. Gnuuuh."

Then there were the guys whose psyches were veritable crazy quilts of sexual confusion. "Gay Whore" was one such fellow. An agitated-looking man, he charged into my booth one night as if his chinos were on fire. Armored in J. Crew and a gold wedding band, he appeared to be a typical suburban husband/daddy looking for some clandestine pussy on a Saturday night.

The first thing he said to me was: "I've been dirty. I've been watching a movie upstairs." (S-World offers an eye-popping selection of coin-operated porno-viewing booths for those who can't be caught renting, i.e., husbands/daddies.)

"Oh really?" I said.

"Guess what kind of movie it was," he said eagerly, as I removed my Target bra and panty set (pink waffle-knit cotton, *tres* jailbait).

Well. What does a square typically consider *dirty?*

---

* Nope!

"Um, was it anal?" I guessed, hoisting my ass into the air to illustrate.

"That's part of it," he said, grinning and masturbating. "It was a bunch of guys."

"Really," said I.

"Oh yeah," he said, producing an illegal inhalant and sniffing ardently. "I love cock. I'm gonna meet a guy later who's gonna fuck me in the ass. And then I'm gonna suck his friend's dick. I love cock more than anything!" he crowed. "I'm a whore."

"You're a huge whore!" I agreed enthusiastically. "A cock-starved whore!"

"Look at my faggot dick," he said, delighted.

"You know," I said, "when you first came in here, I thought you seemed like a respectable family man. But now, it's clear that you're just a dirty, drug-addled homosexual cum-slut!"

As I expected, that did it. He came right away, fueled by his own perceived transgressiveness. Then, he was suddenly all business as he zipped up his flat-front chinos. "That was really good," he said calmly. "Are you here most nights?"

* * *

Without a doubt, the scrutiny of Sex World's female customers was the dolls' heaviest cross to bear. Birds are the worst, man. On Saturday nights, I often had the entire shift to myself. Now, working solo was daunting enough on a ordinary night. Every customer in the store gazed at me in my scarlet terrarium, assessing my weight and worth as if I were the last lobster in the tank at Morton's. However, working alone on a Saturday night was doubly mortifying, because Saturdays meant bachelorette parties. Apparently, blushingly intact Lutheran brides and their attendants think sex shops are an absolute *riot*. They'd canter into the store, knackered on Flirtinis, wearing homemade bachelorette-themed T-shirts and immediately begin giggling over perfectly vanilla movie titles like *Cum Softly, Baby.* (I wondered what they'd think about some of the explicit horse-meets-amputee porn on the Internet.) Inevitably, they'd notice me perched in my X-rated diorama, reading *Psychotic Reactions and Carburetor Dung* and minding my own beeswax. I wasn't sure if they knew I could hear them talking, or if they cared.

"Oh my God. Oh my God, Michelle, there's a girl in there."

"No way. That's a mannequin."

"No, she's totally breathing."

"Oh my God."

"Oh my God!"

"Gross! What does she do? Do they just pay her to sit in there and read?"

"I know! I bet she's supposed to be dancing in there or something."

"She's not that pretty. God. I could do that."

"I dare you to go up there and talk to her."

"Gross! I don't want to go near her!"

And so forth. *You're shit and I'm champagne,* I thought to myself, straightening on the lip-shaped divan. I tried to shrug off the dehumanizing remarks, but girls aren't made of stone. I usually came home on Saturdays, fell into a fitful sleep of back-to-back nightmares and woke up in a blue funk. For the first time, I was losing hit points in the epic battle to maintain my dignity. Girls can be so mean.

Tricks and Hos

Many evenings at the peep show, I worked with a girl named Nico. She was the only black girl employed there, a mother of four with a thick, athletic build and eyes like Scharffenberger chocolate. One night, in a moment of candor, Nico revealed to me that she had once been a full-time hooker and occasionally still turned tricks.

"I promise I won't tell the other girls," I said, excited by this revelation.

"I don't care if you do or you don't," Nico said, sucking the spark out of a freshly ignited Newport. "My whole family knows about it already. Everybody knows." She stretched out on the velveteen chaise like a panther and stared me down.

"I got started when I was eighteen. At the time, I only had one kid, my daughter, who was five. I worked out of the back room of a tanning salon called Polynesian Delight. It was a standard storefront; the tanning beds were in the front and our rooms were in the back."

"How many girls were working there?" I asked, clamoring for details like Brenda Starr, Reporter, trapped in an ill-maintained aquarium.

"Ten or fifteen," Nico said, exhaling a nimbus of smoke. "Mostly white girls, eighteen up to around forty."

"How long did you work there?"

"Until they got popped," Nico said flatly. "Busted by vice. Then, we all worked out of hotel rooms for a year or so." She shrugged. "At least we ate good."

"Did you make a lot of cash?" I asked.

"Oh yeah. God, if I'd known then what I know now, I'd still be sitting on that cash I made when I was eighteen. I'd still have money from prostitution. That's how much hookers make." She sighed. "Plus, she took us out, the woman that ran the place. Got us in everywhere. Nice restaurants. Clubs. I ate out every night."

"I've noticed that a lot of girls in the industry do that," I said, recalling the strippers at Deja Vu who called Hoyt's for swordfish and prime at the merest sign of hunger pangs. "It's like food is a status thing for strippers and whores."

"Yeah. I would order oysters on the half shell. Calamari. I don't even like that shit and I ate it," Nico said, grimacing. Customers passed the window and gawked at us: a girl in a Goth bikini intently questioning a girl in a pink velour tracksuit. Nico's story rushed out of her like a dirty river.

"I'd pay my rent four months at a time because I had nothing better to do with my money," Nico continued. "One day, I called my kid's babysitter and told her to ask my daughter what toys she saw on TV, and write them all down. When I got home, I went out and bought my daughter everything on the list. I could do stuff like that." She snuffed out her cigarette. "It was weird having that kind of money."

"How much did you get for a trick?"

"It depended on a lot of things. At a massage parlor, you can get good money for a half-and-half*, but you have to pay a house fee. I did anal for $400, but I didn't even do it for real. I'd make a fist behind my ass and let them fuck it, or just let them run their dicks up my crack. They couldn't tell I was faking it. Tricks are made to be tricked. That's why they're called that. You trick 'em out of their money."

"What about pimps?" I asked. "Have you ever had one?"

"Let me tell you something crazy about pimps," Nico said with sudden intensity. "A pimp is nothing but a ho, and a ho ain't nothing but a trick. Let me explain: A pimp fucks a ho to get money, but since he's fucking for money, he's a ho. But if a ho fucks a pimp and gives him her money, she's nothing but a trick." Nico laughed at the absurdity of the power structure. "That's why pimps have never had any luck with me. You can't pimp a pimp."

"What's the most you made?" I asked. I remembered the girls I'd met who mysteriously pocketed stacks of crisp hundreds night after night in the clubs.

---

* Half blow job, half sex, much like a pizza with two or more evenly distributed toppings

"I got $4,000 once to meet a guy in Mexico," Nico said proudly. "Four days, a grand a day. All expenses paid. He wouldn't even give me the cash until I got on the return flight, because he didn't want me spending my money on the trip." She grinned. "I also remember one Christmas Eve at the tanning salon. Me and the other girl working each left with $1,500 that night.

"What happened to it?" I asked. "All the money you made?"

"I have no idea," Nico replied, deadpan.

I still had more questions. "Did you ever have a customer who was so revolting that you couldn't make yourself fuck him?"

Nico's cheeks dimpled in amusement. "You can't say no. You can't really turn anyone away when you're in this business. There were these two guys who smelled really bad; we called them Trench Coat Greg and Shitty Booty Jeff. Trench Coat Greg wasn't that bad, actually. He was the first man to eat my pussy and get me off. But Shitty Booty Jeff was the worst. I wouldn't go down on him, just fuck him. Actually, one night, this girl just stared screaming in the hotel room we were sharing. She was supposed to fuck this trick, but his ass was so dirty he left brown streaks on the white sheets. She freaked out."

"Wild," I said. "I couldn't do it, man."

"I'll tell you what," Nico said. "I turned a trick recently and I got physically ill. It's so nasty blowing a guy wearing a condom."

"You're still doing that stuff?"

"Oh yeah. I've fucked Vikings for money. I've done

guys at the club where I dance. Last week, I got a hotel room with this hick, and I pretended to be really naive. I was like, 'Ooh, I don't normally do this! I forgot to bring condoms.' So then, all I had to do was give him a hand job and he paid me. That's the easiest way to trick a trick. Pretend you don't have a condom." Her laugh was brittle. "I even had one guy who offered me $500 to shit on him."

"I'd shit on a dude for five hundy," I remarked. "I mean, I move my bowels for free on a daily basis, right? I might as well turn a profit."

"Right," Nico agreed.

* * *

Since our shift had ended, we swabbed down our booths with alcohol as per the rules. Nico clocked out before me since she was already in her street clothes.

"See you later, masturbator!" she cracked. I waved as she slipped out the secret door into the ladies' room.

The next time I saw Nico, she told me she had been invited to join a trick on a weeklong cruise to Fiji. I congratulated her on this coup, but I never talked to her at length about hooking again. That subject was one of the few taboos in our wee, smoky dollhouse.

Lick It Up

At the Dollhouse, I compiled a veritable field guide of peep-show oddities: customers who defied categorization. Like Harriet the Spy in discount swimwear, I recorded my impressions of all of them in my top-secret slut notebook. From Flashlight Guy, who liked to aim a high-powered Mag-Lite up girls' nostrils and examine their boogies, to Exercise Man, who loved nothing more than watching a girl pant with exertion (I did headstands and fake yoga for him), there was no sexual deviant who escaped my scrutiny.

But one of these specimens achieved near-cult status at Sex World. A frequent customer, he resembled a Malibu Ken doll, complete with a healthy suntan, impeccable Polo wardrobe and an artfully shellacked hank of blonde hair. At first glance, you'd assume he was just another gay financial analyst loose on the streets of Minneapolis. But the instant he entered the store, he transformed into a pie-eyed, insatiable semen-vampire. Cum Licker's mission, ostensibly, was to polish each and every peep show booth to a shine. With his tongue.

My shows with Cum Licker became rather rote after the first couple of times: I'd remove my top (which was really just a formality) while he inspected the booth for cum. If he was lucky, there'd be some ghostly streaks on the glass or a viscous puddle of swimmers on the floor. I would then proceed to talk dirty to Cum Licker while he pawed intently at the cum and asked me questions about how recent it might be, or how many men might have added to it over the course of the evening. He masturbated, but rarely ejaculated. When his ten minutes had ticked down to nothing, he'd beg me to make sure my booth got "extra dirty," and assure me he'd be back once it did. He'd make me promise to keep the janitors at bay, ensuring that the floor would retain its filth. When I rose to exit the booth, he'd assume the down-dog position and lick up the man-chowder.

Cum Licker quickly became famous with peep-show employees and store clerks alike. His jaw-droppingly dangerous habit earned him great notoriety. Everyone was witness to his behavior because he not only "cleaned" the peep-show booths, but he also dutifully lapped the floors of the porn-viewing stations. One night when he finally left the store, a clerk announced "Cum Licker has left the building" over the two-way radio. He was like the Elvis of Sex World.

* * *

The peep show was a fucking circus. Literally. Sex World took its big-top theme to the extreme, right down to

striped tenting and strains of calliope music that burst
from a penis-shaped wishing well at fifteen-minute intervals. Working in the center of that ghastly clownhouse was
taking a toll on my sanity.

Oddly, however, I'd never felt safer at a job than I did
at the Dollhouse.

At the agency, I'd been a professional scapegoat. Every
morning, I'd settle into my cubicle with a tight chest and
an acid stomach. So much shit could go haywire in one
nine-hour day. My boss's boss, an expressionless art nerd
who wore exclusively black, scared the bejesus out of me.
Seriously; I'd rather have faced down a clone army of
Cum Lickers than spend fifteen seconds chatting with this
dude. He was so sober that every status meeting felt like a
baby's funeral. He genuinely cared about the kerning on a
four-color point-of-sale pamphlet. And I sensed he knew
I was bogus, bullshit, an interloper. He knew I did half-
assed work. When I announced I was quitting, he coldly
replied, "I'm not surprised" in his Indo-British accent.

The peep show was different. It was like an artificial
womb. When I was in the booth, I felt like the Dionne
quintuplets in their glass nursery: on display for all, but
ultimately protected. I'd never get in trouble for misplac-
ing a file folder at the peep show or skipping a crucial
conference call to Brazil. I could work drunk, and often
did (until the day I passed out with a cigarette and burned
a hole in the Dollhouse carpet). All I had to do was show
up, take direction and relax certain muscle groups. It was
easy.

Night shifts were weirdly cozy. The same misanthropic

crew of clerks was always present and accounted for. Although the "real employees" generally distrusted the peep-show girls, they'd occasionally banter with me over the two-way radio. There was a collective air of resignation, and a no-future philosophy I found exhilarating. At the end of a shift, I'd peel off my drag and put the wig in my locker. I walked past two strip clubs to get to my car. I imagined the bodies moving behind the tinted windows and felt both nostalgia and remorse about my time as a dancer.

Dollhouse Girls
Don't Have All
the Answers

During the day, I lived a life of stripperly sloth, rising around 10:00, chowing down a bowl of Special K with soy milk and watching insipid dating shows for hours. I didn't do housework or prep meals. I couldn't even be bothered to change out of my jammies until it was absolutely necessary. Around 4:00, I'd bus downtown and meet Jonny for vodka martinis. We'd get plowed on Ketel One and share a basket of cheese curds. Then I'd head down the street, smoking one of the cigarettes to which I'd suddenly become addicted. Life had no aim, which could be righteous or depressing depending on the day.

I worked a static shift at the peep show: six o'clock until shortly past midnight. By the time I'd stashed my "Slim Jane" translucent anal plug in my locker and changed out of my lube-sticky bikini, the remaining dolls would be yawning into their spiked coffee. I remember there was a sign on the wall near my locker that read DOLLHOUSE GIRLS DON'T HAVE ALL THE ANSWERS, posted by our manager in a moment of irritation. The lady was a beat poet and she didn't know it. Her hastily scrawled memos always came out sounding like proverbs.

As I punched out like a knackered factory grunt, the overnight girls filed past me to punch in, a dour skeleton crew with plummy circles beneath their eyes. On the nights I'd done a lot of dildo shows, I affected a bowlegged gait to illustrate the devastation incurred below, a gag that never failed to disgust the girls who were strangely squeamish about our trade.

The head security guard, a beetle-browed medieval-weapons enthusiast, usually walked me to my car while yakking pleasantly about his adventures in mortuary college. Most dolls got a "walk-out," as it was called, to curtail stalkers and the pustulant shitfaced collegiate types who sniffed around the area after dark. (One of the dolls had actually been followed home once, by a customer who was into some really sick B&D shit. She'd managed to evade him, but still recounted the story with a quavering voice.) I never really fretted about being stalked, because I looked almost unrecognizable without my wig. But I still appreciated the walk-outs.

"Did you see a lot of pricks tonight?" asked my temporary bodyguard, my dolly grip.

I always had the same reply: "Dude, my *eyes!*"

* * *

At home, Jonny always woke up to greet me. He'd wrap his arms around me and kiss me with extra tongue, even if I warned him that I was feeling like the communal ass-towel at a Turkish bath. I could hear his smile in the dark as he asked me which freaks I'd serviced that evening.

"Naked Bill Gates," I'd mutter, ticking off the litany on my aching digits. "Frodo Baggins. Exercise Man. Gay whore. Some guy dressed like a nun."

"Really? A plainclothes nun or, like, a Franciscan nun?" Jonny always requested specifics, a quality I appreciated.

"More like a Jesuit nun. You know, modest. Sackcloth and all that."

"Did he have a veil?"

"Yeah, that's how I guessed he was supposed to be a nun."

"Was he naked under his habit?"

"What do you think?"

We'd drift asleep in each other's arms, undisturbed until Peanut inevitably woke up whimpering from a night terror. Jonny was an ace at smoothing Peanut's frayed subconscious; he'd go into her room, lie beside her in bed and sing entire British record albums in a honeyed Liverpudlian tenor until she fell asleep. (Peanut was possibly the only toddler in existence who knew the Rolling Stones's *Their Satanic Majesties Request* album by heart.) Each day she was with us, I watched Jonny draw baths, make kid-friendly breakfasts, tend to bloody noses, kiss oozing boo-boos and explain for the umpteenth time where stepmommies come from. His commitment to Peanut was borderline angelic, and laserlike in its focus.

I knew a lot of guys in town who were divorced fathers and only saw their kids sporadically. No one pilloried them for neglect; guys are notorious for losing interest in their sperm once it exits the vas deferens. But Jonny had successfully fought for three full days a week with Peanut, and he treated each of those days like it was the last time he'd ever stroke her warm, shiny head. So when uncouth outsiders implied that Jonny was a jerk or an unfit father for divorcing Peanut's mom, it incensed me. He worked harder for his child than any father I'd ever observed, hitched or divorced, and I despised seeing him vilified because he'd dared to fall in love with some lost bird from Chicago under less than perfect circumstances.

"Good night, pretty," Jonny would say to me, climbing into bed again after Peanut's sobs had subsided.

" 'Night," I'd reply to the only person who still saw the gold in me.

* * *

My breasts, the very ones I'd cursed as an adolescent for being too small, turned out to be saviors in disguise. They were making money every night; they were keeping us alive. I used my Sex World money to furnish Peanut's bedroom, clothe her in stylish *Dora the Explorer* togs and keep our fridge stocked with luncheon loaf and Juicy Juice. Women have always been known to nourish with their breasts; I saw myself as just another participant in the grand tradition. Our bank account was finally solvent, despite legal bills and spousal maintenance. In a way, I was nursing the whole fucked-up family. This knowledge comforted me in times of strife and tension.

White Christmas

My first holiday season in Minneapolis crept up on me like a drooling sprog in Dr. Dentons. The city was already choking on snow, the roads paved in compacted, dove-gray schmutz. The plows growled all night long, seemingly for recreational purposes, since the snow didn't seem to go anywhere. Still, it was a gorgeous new winter, all sparkling drifts of Bing Crosby fantasy snow. Stainless snow, like the cotton batting that chokes the trunks of Christmas trees. One night I stood outside Sex World and waited in vain for a taxi on the snow-blind avenue. The sidewalk was buried in subzero crystalline fluff, and I couldn't resist doing the old run-n-slide in my purple patent go-go boots. Death spiral! A guy driving his mammoth Escalade down Washington honked at the flying stripper, so I insouciantly flipped him off Italian-style. It used to embarrass me to hang out in front of the store (guilt by association), but not anymore. I was brazen in my wig and leopard-print trench, bikini still on beneath. Anyone who didn't like it could suck a fuck.

A flier appeared in the Dollhouse dressing room inviting all and sundry to the annual Sex World holiday party, which consisted of a walleyed-pike supper (*de rigueur* in Minnesota) and go-kart racing; spouses welcome. I found the idea of porn-store employees and their significant others speeding about in go-karts hilarious. In reality, I imagined it would be a very wholesome affair, when you've spent the entire week alphabetizing fist-fucking videos* and booting sleeping crackheads from video booths, you probably don't feel like tearing it up at the company Christmas party. Fried fish and go-karts are probably just the ticket.

I secretly wished Jonny and I could attend, but the party occured during one of my scheduled shifts, and I decided I'd rather avoid a "discussion" with my unreasonable manager (though I was curious about the husbands and life partners of my fellow tarts-under-glass). As a concession for missing the porn-store shindig (and to celebrate our recent engagement), Jonny and I decided to hit a fully nude juice bar we'd never been to before. The place, enigmatically called Choice, had a reputation for high-mileage, hands-on debauch, and was reportedly raided by cops earlier in the year. Sweet!

Choice was a raucous joint. It was a small, intimate space reminiscent of a Greek restaurant, with gold-painted columns and a fresco of a nighttime scene ama-

---

* The titles of most begin with "F."

teurishly rendered on the wall behind the stage. The girls were wildcats, climbing all over each other onstage and wriggling their blacklight-sensitive tongue studs at the crowd. Every time I dared to place a dollar on the tip rail, I got affectionately molested by the performers onstage. Two of them even yanked my shirt up to my armpits, to the delight of the crowd. "You bad girl! You're not wearing a bra!" one of them exclaimed as she exposed my tits to the crowd. (The strippers were so attentive toward the ladies that one female customer fled the club in embarrassment.) A stripper in a fur-trimmed elf costume dumped a cup of ice cubes down Jonny's pants with an ear-to-ear grin. It was a total riot.

Jonny and I decided to get a double lap dance from a beautiful Hawaiian dancer who had impressed us onstage. She was a perfumed pillar of radiant heat, an island fantasy in an abbreviated Vikings jersey and matching panties. We headed back to the private—lap dance room for the good stuff. She climbed on top of me first, burrowing her head under my shirt and licking my nipples. (I flashed Jonny an ecstatic thumbs-up.) She emerged to grind against my crotch, buffeting my cheeks gently with her warm, augmented breasts, doctoring my closed eyes with miles of fawn-brown cleavage. Bobbing up and down like a carnal mermaid, she wriggled her tongue hard against my carotid artery and bit my earlobe. When my song ended, she turned her attentions to my saucer-eyed fiancé, who was similarly lavished. *Best. Christmas. Pageant. Ever!*

Being at the club as a customer rather than an entertainer reminded me why people were so fascinated with strippers. Some girls had that sweet, spreading warmth, that total generosity of sex and spirit that made even the fortieth customer of the night feel like a coddled VIP. I'd never been able to give that much. It was impossible to imagine myself on the other end of that lap dance, even though I'd done it literally hundreds of times. I'd never had any idea what my customers were feeling. I'd been humping a post all that time, disembodied.

* * *

Since Sex World was open 365 days a year, my manager informed me I had to work either Christmas Eve or Christmas Day. Hilarious. I chose not to work Christmas Eve, since it had considerably more of that "O Holy Night" magic 'n' mojo. I wanted to play Ms. Santa Claus (ho!) to my soon-to-be-stepdaughter on the night before Christmas, and I also wanted to see what kind of people come to a peep show on Christmas Day. Some of the girls wore appropriately themed costumes when they worked holidays. I told everyone I was going as myrrh.

Back in Black

After four months of flogging my increasingly unresponsive genitalia at the Dollhouse, I found myself desiring,
nay, *panting* to strip onstage again. I missed the eye of the
storm, the poles and the panty auctions and the threat of
raids by vice. The evening Jonny and I had spent stageside
at the little jack shack had left me wondering if I could
ever be as fully engaged as the stripper who'd knocked us
senseless. She was like a bottomless Jedi master, the per-
sonification of the reason why live nude girls exist in the
first place. I hadn't sensed her pain or her exhaustion or
anything festering inside that gorgeous shell. There was
no evidence pointing to the young son I later found out
she had. Just pure charismatic heat rising under the seven
veils, a ylang-ylang-scented tower of power. Could I tap
into that cask of delirium-inducing sexmagick? When I'd
danced before, I'd tried to disguise my weak corporate
butt as a bona fide candy ass. This time, there'd be no
hiding. I would become what I wanted to be, sweeten my

whole deal until I was irresistable to dudes. Flies to honey;
my latest mantra.

In February, I found out that Choice, the club Jonny
and I had visited, was holding auditions. I was working at
Sex World that night, but I knew I could escape the Barbie
box for an hour or two. There was something appropriate
about resuscitating my stripping career at the very joint
that had inspired me to do so. So at eight o'clock sharp, I
waved good-bye to the cashiers, pulled on a pair of jeans
and a faux-fur bolero over my bikini, and left the Dollhouse vacant (a mortal sin for a Doll, but I didn't care).
The entertainment district in Minneapolis is as wee and
precious as Mister Rogers' Neighborhood; I only needed
to cross the street to audition.

Choice was dark and mostly empty; early evenings are
downtime for most strip clubs. Still, the rubber plants,
tented jury-rigged rooms and twinkling fairy lights created an atmosphere of low-budget coziness that I found
quite pleasant. I filled out a brief questionnaire, requested a couple of tunes at the DJ booth and watched as a
coltish, ponytailed thing auditioned in sandals.

When I was summoned to the stage, I did a two-song
Rolling Stones set, cheered on by Nico, who'd accompa-
nied me for (im)moral support. The stage was banana-
slick, as the girl who auditioned before me had coated her
hindquarters in sesame oil and rolled around on the floor
like an epileptic sun worshipper. However, I was able to
execute a few of my signature kung-fu kicks and drum
punches, much to the delight of the strippers clustered
around the tip rail. I was also the only auditioning girl

who bothered to work the pole, and I did so with gusto. My Bettie Page wig seems to inspire chutzpah; whenever I wear it, I'm like Popeye on iron supplements. As "Beast of Burden" faded out, I crouched to collect my tips and was pleased to see that I'd amassed a substantial pile of cash for a Monday night. As I left the stage, I felt completely energized. I was back, man!

Afterward, the general manager, a former stripper in slouchy suede boots and a pair of silicon antiques, asked to speak to me. She told me that she'd just fired a girl for fucking a customer in the VIP room, and offered me a job on the day shift. "You were good," she told me. "You have the kind of body that men like." It was the first time I'd ever been the recipient of positive feedback from management about my dancing or image. A good omen, I reasoned.

* * *

I started working at the club two days later. (My manager at the Dollhouse snorted and hung up on me when I timidly informed her I was leaving.) I didn't bother with costumes (save my black Bettie wig) or a goony stage name; I simply went as myself and worked alone, projecting nothing but the hilarious illusion that I was the axis of the sexual universe. I whispered in dudes' ears. I touched their chests and legs and necks and and didn't automatically reel. I played the girlfriend. I pulled them close so they could smell the Stella McCartney I'd dabbed on my pulse points. I deep-sixed the librarian act, shut my smart mouth and rode them like ponies at the Preakness. *Ram-a-lam-a-lam.*

Suddenly, they all stood up when I seized their hands. I made over $1,000 within my first three days. I'd figured it out. Riddle solved. Case cracked. I felt like I'd graduated, only instead of "Pomp and Circumstance," the band played Warrant.

I just needed to be dumb, sometimes in both senses of the word.

* * *

My relative success at Choice eventually made me a target for stripperly ire and the subject of much dished dirt; hell, I was everyone's mud-flap girl. I'd never been hated at a club before, but I realized that was because I had never made money before. New girls are never popular, really. At a normal job (say, at a tax-preparation firm, women's clinic, petting zoo or advertising agency), new employees are greeted with curiosity, courtesy and, in some cases, deference in the guise of freshly baked brownies. At a strip joint, however, a new girl might as well don veal underwear and dance the Watusi through a gauntlet of jackals. Most veteran strippers are punch-drunk on Haterade, and they'd sooner dredge their Vuitton clutch in a cow pie before mustering a pixel of common courtesy toward their fellow woman.

I learned to keep to myself, and it served me well. Instead of yakking and popping uppers in the dressing room with the other day girls, I lurked patiently on the floor and logged every move the customers made. I learned to sense when they were ready for me, or for anyone; I imagined them as ripening apples slowly heading into the red. Then I'd descend. "Hi, sweetie. You look ready."

Since I was now determined to take stripping seriously, I determined it was time to attain a quasi-exotic, noncarcinogenic tan. Strippers must be tan. A proper suntan (whether authentic or phony) conceals cellulite, enhances the complexion and lends one a burnished *Girls Gone Wild*—esque aura of health, wealth and desirability. Coco Chanel knew it. I finally acknowledged it.

First, I tried using self-tanning foam. This resulted in streaky, tangelo-colored flesh—I resembled a jaundiced infant rather than a sun-kissed goddess. I decided to seek professional help in the form of spray tanning, a relatively new technology that involves being hosed down with an industrial-strength darkening agent in a claustrophobic facility. Spray tanning is scary. You slowly asphyxiate in a booth while automated jets douse your naked body with a chilly amber mist. It's alarmingly noisy, and for some reason, the whole process made me want to pee. You must take pains to shield your palms from the spray (assuming the approved "spray-tan stance") and coat your ashy toes and knuckles with "barrier cream" (which, I suspect, is simply hand lotion.)

A spray tan takes around twelve hours to develop, which means that you can hit the pillow a translucent, blue-white lass and wake up looking like a Cosby kid. Brilliant! I "tanned" three times the first week, and gradually went from Sondra to Rudy. At work, I danced with an extra switch in my hips. It felt delicious to be fortified with bogus melanin, and my skin didn't glow under black-light anymore.

Such physical renovations were necessary to compete at Choice. Most of the strippers there were extra-tasty ("Best-looking day shift in town," the owner of the club boasted to me once). There was Veronica, whose drum-tight ass bobbled hypnotically as she traveled from table to table. There was Sinnamon, whose breasts were nearly the size of regulation basketballs and certainly as pneumatic. Little Courtney looked exactly like Pamela Anderson plus ten years and spontaneous dwarfism (close enough for her legions of devout customers). One girl had even had cheek implants, proof of a commitment to self-improvement that garnered silent respect from even the most enthusias-tic scalpel-junkies. And I could never forget Coco, a sweet drunk with tattooed eyeliner and lipstick and a Chicago ac-cent that rivaled my mother's. They were all lifers, the kind of gals who work in the industry until they're hauled off to the dementia cottage at Olde Oakes Convalescent Facility. I admired their gumption and their scars.

The day girls at Choice liked barbecues. During a stretch of unseasonably warm days in April, they dragged a Weber grill into the parking lot and cooked up piles of chicken wings, whooping at their own ingenuity. Passing cars on Second screeched to a halt at the sight of fifteen half-naked women gnawing on chicken in broad daylight. They even kept their platforms on.

"I'm going to get arrested for this," the manager moaned as the girls fanned the smoke and giggled, their faces aged in the sunlight.

* * *

Because the day shift tended to attract more seasoned perverts than green curiosity seekers, I got to know a lot of customers very well. There was a foot-obsessed publishing executive who came in three times a week to massage the girls' bunions and pull their toes. He liked my manky feet a lot because they supposedly reeked the most of anyone's.

"I'll give you money for your video game if you let me pull those icky toes for fifteen minutes," he'd offer hopefully as I pumped quarters into the Playboy Match* machine in the back of the club.

"Deal," I'd say, extending my foot graciously in his direction. Point, flex, ka-ching. Too bad we didn't have any paying slots; I'd probably be downing lime rickeys in Barbados by now.

Another regular was a computer engineer from Nigeria who claimed I exemplified his ideal woman: a friggin' hulk.

"So strong!" he crowed once. "You are so thick and so strong. Such muscles! You are big, big, big!"

"I am not," I replied. "I'm a delicate lotus flower."

"No," Nigerian Man repeated. "You are so big. Wow, big legs and hips!"

"I hate you," I said sincerely. I was in the best shape of my life thanks to that fucking pole, and this guy was acting like I was Gilbert Grape's mama.

---

* The greatest bar game ever. It's like playing Memory, except with boobs.

"I saw a show on television the other day," Nigerian Man said, switching gears abruptly. "A show with a woman called Oprah."

"I think I've heard of her," I said drily.

"Big women are so wonderful! I truly think you are my friend," Nigerian Man insisted. "My true friend. Like big college buddy."

My least favorite regulars were the assclowns who insisted on wearing parachute pants *sans* underwear to the club for maximum stimulation during lap dances. You could feel every wrinkle on their cock during a prolonged session, and they'd often pause the dance to "adjust." Some of them even wore condoms beneath their *loserhosen,* and after a private dance, they'd discreetly pull off their used Trojan Micron and shove it between the couch cushions. Later, some poor girl would find the drenched latex treat and shudder. The manager would be summoned to retrieve it, and arrive wearing rubber gloves and a defeated expression. I wished those men would stay home and hire prostitutes, rather than coming into the club and demanding high-friction dances. But when I explained this to one of them in exasperation, he told me that it was more exciting to get off in a forbidden environment. He liked to see the girlies squirm. Yuck.

I encountered my share of unique fetishes as well; Sex World didn't have a monopoly on kinks in Mill City. One man came into the club on two separate occasions and asked me to punch him in the stomach and testicles as hard as I could for ten solid minutes. He explained that he'd been raped as a child, and that being jacked in the gut reminded him of the incident and, in turn, aroused him on a subconscious level. I'd never hit anyone, but I pummeled the shit out of this poor man per his specific instructions.

"Ooh, you fucking bitch," he'd squeal in a little boy's voice.

"You can trust me, sweetie," I'd say in a sickeningly phony voice, caressing his tense jaw. "I won't hurt you." Then, *bam!* I'd bust him in the junk.

It wasn't as funny as it sounds. After he left the first time, I couldn't stop shaking for an hour. Certain people give strippers so much power that they sometimes short-circuit.

The best customers were the ones who attained strip-club nirvana, a state identifiable by a blissed-out smile and a slouching posture on the lap couch. They're seeing the light, baby. Once I gave twelve dances in a row to a Buddhist businessman who beamed like a pageant queen and didn't move except to nod emphatically when I asked him if he wanted another dance.

"You are like the goddess Athena," he murmured as I brushed the length of my torso along his cheek. "When you talk about media criticism, it gives me an instant hard-on."

My kind of customer.

But nothing lasts forever in the strippersphere.

Motoring

Though I doggedly tried to ignore my gut feeling, all signs pointed to encroaching burnout. I knew I wasn't going to be a nudie cutie forever; I was already on the ripe-to-rotten end of the age spectrum. It was obvious that my breaking point was fast approaching. I didn't know when I'd finally snap, but I acknowledged the inevitability of the event. I'd been getting some freelance work at the local alternative weekly, which meant I could plausibly be a paid writer instead of a paid dickwarmer. I entertained these thoughts most nights when I came home exhausted and soaked my bruised body in a hot bath. Jonny could always be counted on to hang out tubside and listen to me crab about the day's indignities.

"Peanut and I had a good time tonight," he'd say. "We went to the comic shop, and then we came home and colored for a few hours."

"Sounds wholesome," I'd say, cranky. "I spent my evening bartering with a Mexican guy who wanted to pay $50 for my rag-stained Kiss undies."

"Well, did you sell them?"

"Hell no! How else am I going to get Peter Criss's face on my crotch?"

"I can't believe Peter Criss is your favorite."

On D-day, which was a Wednesday, I sat at the bar drinking a foul cocktail of cranberry and pineapple juice from the beverage gun. Onstage, there was a blonde with a heart-shaped ass dancing to "Barbie Girl" by the Swedish group Aqua. Actually, she was sort of marching back and forth in her hip-high vinyl boots, tipping her defiant little chin at anyone who looked at her sideways. I noticed a table of bored strippers watching her contemptuously. The girl had a leaden gait and and an advanced case of bitchface, but she did look like Barbie incarnate, and that was reason enough for the others to hate her. Even on a bad day, a yellow-headed bitch could mint, and this incensed the ethnic contingent. Plus, she had a fan club composed of dirty old retirees who paid big bucks to "feel her boobies," as one of the men informed me as he waited for her one morning.

The Aqua-torture ended, and the girl left the stage to get felt up by her senile minions. Business was brisk that day, and there were customers seated in every corner of the club, rejecting and accepting lap dances at will. A lot of strippers had shown up to work that afternoon, and the manager was still turning some away at the door. It was one of those days where there's a subaudible buzz in the air and the club feels like a honeycomb crawling with drones. I should have put on my game face and seized the opportunity to make some money during what had been a slow week. I hadn't had a dance yet, and it was two o'clock, prime time for hustling.

And yet, I couldn't get up.

I could not get up. I heard the other dancers trying out their lines all around me. "Want company?" "Ready to play?" "Wanna dance?" (and the enterprising "Are you ready to go to paradise?" frequently intoned by a dancer named Paradise). The room was filled with their phony geisha chirping. More girls emerged from the dressing room in pairs and threesomes, splitting off like mitochondria to shill for their supper. So many of them, all enemies by necessity. It was like a local beauty pageant that never ended, with fresh delegates arriving daily from as far away as Wisconsin. I didn't blame the girls for hating each other anymore. I was actually surprised no one had been killed.

I'd always believed in the potency of women. I'd supported and participated in the sex industry even as it was buffeted with criticism from people who felt it objectified us. I'd felt like such a libertine dancing onstage to AC/DC or masturbating in a glass box for some civil engineer. I argued with any well-meaning friend who dared to insinuate that I was devaluing myself. There was a reason men paid ridiculous sums of money for the company of an exaggeratedly feminine creature. Because strippers are spectacular. They rule.

It wasn't the nudity or the grinding or any sex-phobic moral issue that was pinning me to my chair in a moment of blinding epiphany. It was actually the opposite. The one-on-one aspects of the industry made sense; it was the whole girls-in-bulk thing that repulsed me. Hundreds of girls on the floor at some clubs, all reduced to begging dogs for an army of smug little emperors. The rules of attraction were reversed at a strip club. Girls that could halt midday traffic at Nicollet Mall were rejected by fat guys wearing Zubaz. Joe Punchcard with $20 could toy with several dancers over the course of an afternoon, finally selecting the one who'd receive the dubious privilege of entertaining him for three and a half minutes. The rejected girls, regardless of how loved they were by husbands or paramours or infants at home, would feel worthless for an instant, and all because of ol' Joe. Those instances multiplied, and soon everyone felt like creeping crud, regardless of how much ego they projected.

It's like a girl buffet, and no one really savors the brown goop at a buffet. You pile your sanitized plate with discount food and shovel it in as quickly as you can. It all tastes the same and has a sluggish mouth-feel. You don't stop to weigh the relative merits of the chicken versus the spaghetti. You don't notice the orphaned lo mein noodle in your blueberry cobbler. It's all crap, but it does the job. There's always more food somewhere, another steam tray being hustled out from the kitchen.

I hated the the girl buffet. *I deserve better presentation,* I thought. We all did.

I still couldn't stand up. I wiggled my toes, but my legs wouldn't cooperate. It was like the dial-up connection between my brain and my body had timed out. My chest tightened, and I could suddenly hear my heart playing a brutal Rick Allen fill. And then I started bawling.

In the bathroom, I called Jonny. "I gotta get out of here," I blubbered.

"What's wrong?" he asked, alarmed.

"I don't know," I said. "I just can't do this anymore."

"What do you want to do?"

"Anything else, man."

"I thought you liked stripping. Isn't that why you're still there?" he asked.

"Was," I said, taking off my thong, using it to wipe the tears and eyeliner and weepy schmutz off my cheeks and stuffing it into my backpack.

"I *was* here."

* * *

I'd hit the wall hard. It had been a year since I'd walked into Schieks dressed like a waitress—short-haired, knock-kneed in my new stilettos, looking like Dorothy Hamill learning to walk on solid ground after seventeen hours at the rink. Now, I looked at myself in the bathroom mirror. Hair extensions down to my waist. Fake tan. A faceful of MAC stage makeup. Acrylic talons, studded with anxious tooth imprints that betrayed my neuroses. Streaks of bronzer on my sternum to create trompe l'oeil cleavage. I didn't even recognize myself. I only saw a tough stripper who looked like she might punch my face.

I limped over to my manager, a sweet man who listened to Sam Kinison records to exorcise the demon of his bitter divorce, and begged off work for the day.

"No problem," he said. "I've got too many girls today."

I walked down the street, sobbing into my sleeve. I'm not usually one to cry, but the force of the revelation had pulverized me inside. I got in my car and drove all the way out to the house that Jonny and I had bought the week before, a sixties rambler on a tree-lined street in a small town that none of our friends had heard of. We hadn't moved in yet, but the lawn was Levittown green and the facade of the house looked bright and inviting. Looking up at that little white shack in the suburbs, our own slice of *Brady Bunch* equity, I thought to myself: *the house that jacking-off built.*

It was true. Were it not for a veritable army of erect penises in the warehouse district, I wouldn't have been standing on the berm, staring up at my first house. Back at the apartment, there was a Bettie Page lunch box atop the refrigerator; most people assumed it was merely ornamental kitsch, but it was actually filled with thousands of dollars in cash. I'd never been able to sock away that kind of money when I was a salaried employee in a legitimate field. Stripping had pummeled me bloody, but it had also stroked me and spoon-fed me and twisted its tongue in my eustachian tube.

But my gap year, my little *rumspringa,* was over. It was time to go back to the real world.

Stephanie Says

In stripper-ese, "retirement" can mean a couple of things. Usually, it refers to leaving the sex trade for a square job (see also: "going clean" and "getting off the pole"). In a few lucky cases, it refers to literal retirement from the workforce. I'd heard successful girls bragging about how they'd socked away half a mil and were planning to move to an ambigious region of Minnesota referred to as "up North" and breed Lipizzan horses for the rest of their days. Other times, retirement meant meeting a moneyed bachelor, moving into his mansion on Lake of the Isles, getting fat and becoming a stay-at-home mom to a passel of adorable future strippers. Neither of these options was realistic in my case, but I needed to keep myself in booze and cookies somehow.

Unemployed, fairly unemployable and facing a thirty-year mortgage, I made the snap decision to become a phone-sex girl. You can't beat the flexibility of that gig; successful phone girls boast about long, lazy days spent watching *General Hospital* while moaning half-assedly into a headset. Besides, after the five months I'd spent coaxing sperm out of inebriated bums at Sex World ("Come on, you can do it! I think I see a bead of pre-jack!), I assumed I'd be a natural at phone-fuck a go-go.

Scoring the job was cake; after a brief audition with a company in Alabama, I was offered a full-time position. ("I'm really into S&M," the kindly soccer mom who hired me confided. "My husband and master, Kevin, just bought me a new collar.") I was mailed a disarmingly stodgy orientation packet that explained how to deal with various calls, and it was one of the funniest bits of unintentional comedy I have ever read. Seriously, it was *brilliant.* For example: "*Black and Married*: If you receive a call of this nature, you should pretend to be a large-breasted black woman. (Do not attempt to 'sound black' by affecting an accent or using jive talk.) Your husband is a truck driver or businessman, and he is rarely home. You are very horny and enjoy anal sex. Be sure to mention your large, chocolate-colored nipples."

Or this classic item: "*Redhead*: If you receive the 'Redhead' prompt, tell the caller you have red hair *everywhere*!" I mean, why was the verbiage so coy? The only people reading the thing are prospective phone-sex operators, so why not just say, "You have a flaming-red cooze that could singe the retinas of observers. You look as if you're in the crowning stage of giving birth to Carrot Top. Call the fire department, Miss Thing, because your pussy is ABLAZE!" I wondered why I hadn't gotten a job as an internal copywriter with the company instead. I could have written far superior orientation materials.

I quickly had our new house equipped with a second phone line, and Jonny bought me a nice papasan chair so I could recline comfortably while entertaining my callers. (Unlike many phone-sex jobs, where operators receive calls at their leisure, I had to log in and remain tethered to the phone for my entire shift.) I couldn't wait to act "Black and Married," or to assume any of the other twelve-odd personae that callers could request. You can imagine my disappointment when I realized that a staggering majority of phone-sex customers opted for the "Barely Legal" option. Due to popular demand, I was forced to invent "Stephanie" and remain in character for up to eight hours a night.

"Stephanie" was a teenage virgin who lived at home with her wealthy, frequently absent parents. She had dark blonde hair, green eyes, a voice like a slightly less-cerebral Joey Lauren Adams, 34C breasts, and a libido that raged like Dylan Thomas on his deathbed. She enjoyed tanning in her bra and panties, especially when she suspected her male neighbors were watching. (Aside from baiting voyeurs, "Stephanie" only had two other hobbies: reciprocal cunnilingus with her best friend, Kimberly, and, of course, phone sex.) Callers went bananas for Stephanie. She was so popular that I often found myself answering the phone, "Hello (giggle), this is Stephanie!" up to twenty times a shift. Oh, how I grew to hate Stephanie. I secretly hoped she'd grow up, get fat and smoke until her voice coarsened to a growl. Meanwhile, my callers grew increasingly enamored.

"Way to go!" my shift supervisor Andrea enthused on

the phone one night. "You're doing great. Your average call-hold time is seven minutes!"

"The only calls I ever get are 'Barely Legal,'" I complained. "Can't you direct some of the 'Hispanic Amputee' calls to my extension?"

"'Barely Legal' is our most popular offering," Andrea said in her Splenda-sweet Southern drawl. "Men like 'em young, dumb an' thirsty for cum."

"I guess," I said, but I was disillusioned. The sex industry had ceased to be novel. I was going to have to do the unimaginable: get a straight job.

* * *

Armed with a mostly fabricated résumé, I somehow finagled a job as a claims examiner at an insurance company in the suburbs. It was a typical Orwellian cube farm, with each employee neatly parceled into a dove-gray compartment. This place was *soooo* square, in terms of both corporate climate and the workspace itself. It was so square it existed in the fifth dimension. I worked in a tesseract. My boss was a fastidious woman whose amusing diction and passive hostility embodied every stereotype about Minnesota. She forbade me to use the Internet for personal business (bogus!), but she did reward me when I behaved. For instance, when I occasionally performed beyond the scope of my assigned duties, she'd bring me a roll of candy and a laser-printed certificate that read "You're a Lifesaver!" And so began my life as an upstanding citizen and lifesaver to the dimmest of stars.

A Stripper
Was Born

Most sex workers (a classification that includes strippers) cite a past incident of sexual abuse in trying to explain the illicit path they've stumbled upon. I have no such justification. I was never molested as a child, probably because I wasn't very attractive. Though my mother did her best to outfit me in the preppy armor of the era, I always looked disheveled and owlish. I had obsessive-compulsive disorder and facial tics. My gray eyes shrank behind oversized, Plexiglas-thick spectacles, and my teeth were fenced in by a glittering array of modern orthodontia (retainers, space maintainers, braces, all composed of silver wire, acrid cement and/or tongue-colored dental acrylic). I wasn't a dimpled, curly-haired Campbell Kid ripe for diddling by an older relative. In fact, if I'd been called upon to endorse a product, it probably would have been a set of junior encyclopedias. Or bulk birdseed. Something boring. The point is, my formative years were entirely free of sexual trauma.

That said, I'm not sure how I became a stripper and my brother became a misguided man-child with a jones for cocaine. Those kinds of fates are supposed to be reserved for kids of "broken" homes, kids who are reared on factory wages and whose lives are a pastiche of fake stepfathers, mobile homes and government dairy. By contrast, Marc and I were raised by an indivisible couple (Mom and Dad were both way too uncool to divorce).

Like many children in our tiny suburb of Chicago, I went to Catholic school, complete with daily Mass, ancient nuns in dark habits, box-pleated jumpers, corporal punishment and the constant reassurance from my elders that I was going to sizzle like suet in hell. It was a fairly typical academic experience for Catholic children in the 1950s; however, this was the eighties. I was one of the last generations of American kids to receive a traditional, pre-Vatican II religious education, and predictably, it fucked me up and made me slutty.

My home life, by contrast, was idyllic. We had a big house in a bucolic subdivision, complete with a finished basement, yards of blue Cookie Monster shag and a much-envied wet bar stocked with dessert liqueurs. My dad, a successful restaurateur at the time, drove a cherry Corvette with vanity plates. My older brother, Marc, and I were coddled to the point of asphyxiation. We vacationed in Orlando, wore infinite layers of Benetton and consumed enough steak dinners to give the average kid iron poisoning. Except for a gory incident around the time *Gleaming the Cube** was released, in which I wiped out on a Nash skateboard, my childhood was a stainless suburban ideal.

When we weren't tearing down Eureka Street on our Schwinn tandem bike, my brother and I hung out at the Matterhorn, the German supper club my parents and grandmother owned. The Matterhorn was huge, gloriously tacky and, according to my father, a bitch to heat and cool. When you walked in the front door, there was a stone grotto with a tank that housed a single suicidal catfish, and a gift shop stocked with stuffed toys and Black Forest gummies. An immense moose head was mounted above the fireplace in the main dining room, and busboys could always be counted on to lodge lit cigarettes in the moose's mouth.

At Christmas, a human-sized animatronic snowman came out of storage to greet diners in the foyer. My aunts poured Manhattans behind the bar, and an eccentric organist performed every Saturday in the banquet room. (My brother and I were obsessed with the organist because he had a wet-look Jewfro, a porno mustache and a Clapper-equipped bachelor pad.) The waitresses, hefting trays of prime rib and sauerbraten, wore bodices that crimped their waists and made them look like aging St. Pauli Girls. They cooed gamely over my brother and I, even though we were unattractive children with chapped lips.

---

* The zenith of eighties thrash cinema, starring a young, pre–domestic battery Christian Slater

The Matterhorn was a big Mafia draw. My grand-mother, a take-no-shit Leo who ruled the joint with a heavily bejeweled fist, ordered the prettier waitresses to entertain the various mob heavies who haunted the supper hour. The girls, dour but obedient, would cozy up in a booth and drink Dom with whichever coterie of gangsters had shown up to dine that day. My grandmother knew that this kind of socializing was vital to the success of her crum-bling bierhall. The waitresses were aware they were being pimped, but there was something flattering about sharing a magnum with Lucky or Pancakes or whomever had just been released from the state clink and felt like celebrating with bad music and Kraut food. The Matt was not unlike a strip club in this regard. I often think Grandma would have made a first-rate titty-bar proprietor.

Don't get me twisted; those were wholly innocent times. GUT ESSEN, GUT TRINKEN read an antique placard above the dining-room entrance. No one in the family was able to translate this, as my clan was neither German nor intellectual, but I suspected it meant something about good eats and fulfillment. Indeed, my family was well nourished in every regard.

We lived in the same rock-solid brick manor for the entirety of our childhoods, and we graduated from state universities. At that point, we were expected to connect the dots and move onto lucrative, satisfying jobs in the corporate sector. Marc bailed early on and became a ca-reer waiter; I held on a few more years doing administra-tive "girl" jobs in a series of downtown high-rises. I typed memos, brewed coffee and fretted over whether I'd ever be promoted to Assistant Junior Micro Flyspeck Account Coordinator. Naturally, my folks were delighted. It wasn't until I moved to Minnesota that I began to reconsider my kid-tested, parent-approved lifestyle as a white-collar grunt.

* * *

I don't know what my first exposure to stripping was. As a curious kid, I was vaguely aware that nude dancers existed, but my mental image of them was inexplicably corny and burlesque, rather than overtly sexual. (Maybe I'd watched the strip-club scene in *The Graduate* where poor, chaste Elaine Robinson snivels at the sight of tasseled pasties.) Later on, I saw strippers on the trashy talk shows that dominated my freon-cooled summer afternoons circa 1989, but I never imagined myself doing such a thing for money. Those broads were toothless and shrill; they threw chairs and sobbed until fjords of blue-black mascara stained their cheeks. There was nothing sexy or intriguing about that. Stripping seemed desperate, the provenance of the chronically unfortunate.

Things are different now that stripper-chic has infiltrated youth culture. As of 2004, modest gym bunnies can take "cardio strip" classes and tone their glutes while fulfilling a transgressive fantasy. Teenage girls wear *Hustler* logo hoodies and spray-tan themselves into Gold 'n' Plump splendor. Feminists, brainiacs and "alternative" types are peeling their Elizabethan corsets off on Web sites like Suicide Girls and Nekkid Nerds. Coeds lift their shirts and squeal for spring-break sexploitation pictorials.

Sexual exhibitionism is the norm, not the deviation. But when I was a teenager in the era when punk broke, no self-respecting riot grrl (save Courtney Love, a vocal alumnus of several strip clubs) would have mooned a crowd for cash tips. We cocooned ourselves in flannel and neglected our hair. We railed against ozone pollution, Ticketmaster service charges and impossibly proportioned fashion dolls. Becoming a stripper would have been an unthinkable waste of our so-called lives.

* * *

The first time I gave critical thought to stripping as a profession, I was nineteen years old and attending college in Iowa City, a town that prides itself on being the lone follicle of *hoch kultur* in the dank armpit that is Iowa. I routinely got my hair cut at a punk salon downtown, and all the hairdressers there were rowdy tattooed hellcats who looked like they'd just ponied out of a hot-rod magazine. One day, during a haircut, one of them revealed to me that she occasionally danced at Dolls, a strip club in the neighboring town of Coralville.

"Do you make good money?" I asked her as she sheared my hair into a reasonable facsimile of Winona Ryder's late-nineties pixie cut.

"Yeah, the money is awesome," she enthused, reaching over me to crank the volume on the *Natural Born Killers* soundtrack. "You should try it."

"Really?" I said, stunned. "Do you think I could?"

"Definitely," she said. "You're the right type. I can loan you a pair of my shoes if you want to audition."

I laughed. "I don't think I could. I'm too chicken." I was secretly flattered that this *uber*cool Nancy Spungen look-alike thought I could be a stripper, but at the same time, the idea seemed ridiculous. I decided to keep my day job doing Dutch-language data entry at the library.

* * *

So when—*why*—did my little red Corvette veer onto the freeway of indecency? I think I've finally got it sussed. Most girls get into stripping because they've discovered a fast crowd, are mired in financial woe or have lived with dysfunction for so long that they're naturally drawn to the fucked-up family dynamic in strip clubs. For me, it was the polar opposite. I had spent my entire life choking on normalcy, decency and Jif sandwiches with the crusts amputated. For me, stripping was an unusual kind of escape. I had nothing to escape from but privilege, but I claimed asylum anyway. At twenty-four, it was my last chance to reject something and become nothing. I wanted to terrify myself. Mission accomplished.

Coda

You, the reader, are hoping to find some sort of redemption in this sprawling epic (okay, sprawling pamphlet) of a corporate yes-girl who literally puts her ass on the line and becomes a sex worker for sport. I'm afraid you won't find any here. That's the deal with true stories; they rarely deliver on a climactic level. Especially when the story is about something as puddle-shallow and symbolically molecular as stripping. *Girl goes wild.* That's all she wrote. For the curious, Jonny and I did get married, and we're the happiest cats in the whole U.S.A. Peanut was a gorgeous flower girl. We live in the 'burbs, and no one strips unless they're taking a bubble bath.

I will admit that I was permanently altered by my time living among the strippers in their moist, humid habitat. I underwent a chemical change as well as a physical transformation. I dinged up my femurs on the pole and was suddenly gifted with a pair of bad knees. My feet, like Barbie's, are practically stuck in a tortured high-heel silhouette. (On the plus side, pole work gave me abs of adamantium.)

I wrote this because I never could have let all of this psychic detritus percolate inside of me forever. Some stories beg to be told (narrator's rule of thumb: Any story involving a panty auction is *required* to be told). So I spilled it. I hope you were adequately entertained, and I hope the periodic waves of nausea were tempered by at least an occasional *frisson* of enjoyment.

* * *

What is it about that damned pole, anyway? Some girls assault it, some girls ignore it, some girls hitch a ride on it and spin. Doesn't really matter; it takes all kinds to entertain. I went from regarding the pole as an adversary (like Charlie Brown's kite-noshing tree) to eventually scaling it with quick, calloused thighs. The last time I took the stage, I climbed the pole, hung upside down like a naked fruit bat and waved at the crowd. From that perspective, the place looked almost normal. That, friends, means it's time to come down. I righted myself and slid to my feet, bruised but otherwise smashing.